EXPAT

ENTREPREN

EXPAT ENTREPRENEUR

How To Create and Maintain Your Own Portable Career Anywhere In The World

JO PARFITT

First Published In Great Britain 2006

by www.BookShaker.com

Edited by: Laura Markey, Rebecca Law, Charlotte Eichler, Zoe Meyer and Sally Edwards

Typeset in Century Schoolbook

Praise for Expat Entrepreneur

"This terrific book is exactly the support I could have done with on our overseas postings and even on my return to the UK. Parfitt has gathered together her own insights and experience and that of many other entrepreneurial expats to create an indispensable tool for anyone wanting to create something new wherever they land."

Bobby Meyer, publisher, Sage Press
Serial entrepreneur and three times expatriate, author of 'Topiary Inspiration' and many other titles.
www.sagepress.co.uk

"One of the best books there is for expatriates who want a career adventure. As she has demonstrated in all of her wonderful books for expats, Jo Parfitt really knows her stuff. This book is packed with examples, tips and of course, lots of inspiration. Don't forget to pack it before you set off on your new life."

Robin Pascoe, expat expert and author of 'Moveable Marriage', 'Homeward Bound' and other titles.
www.expatexpert.com

I would like to acknowledge the following individuals for their help with sourcing and compiling the case studies: Rebecca Law, Laura Markey, Jayne Lillywhite, Christine Rolland, Val Tucker, Kari Thingvold, Ruth Rusby, Sally Edwards, Lois Levett, Adam O' Riordan and Charlotte Eichler.

Acknowledgements

Thanks to Ian, my husband, cheerleader and soulmate, without whom I would never have embarked on this adventure overseas. I often think back to how I felt in 1987, when he was already based in Dubai and we were planning our wedding. How I begged him to come home and start our new life together in England.

'If you don't come to Dubai, you will regret it for the rest of your life,' he said.

He was right.

Thanks too, to all those many people who have contributed to this book, either with proof–reading, interviewing or writing. This book could never have been written, however, without the generosity of all the expatriate entrepreneurs who were willing to talk to us and share their secrets.

About the author

In 1987 after her marriage to Ian, Jo Parfitt found herself thrown into the role of 'trailing spouse'. Over the next ten years Jo lived in Dubai, Oman and Norway. From 1997 to 2004 she was back in England before moving to The Netherlands.

Never one to be idle, Jo is passionate about maintaining a professional identity despite countless changes in country, lifestyle and opportunity. Much of her time has been spent creating and maintaining her own mobile career and she has become an authority on the subject of dual and portable careers. Expatriate Entrepreneurs is the result of the many opportunities Jo has seized and the countless inspiring individuals she has met along the way, who were willing to share their success stories and their secrets in this book.

Going overseas can be the catalyst for a sea–change in your career. Opportunities that existed in one country may dry up in another. Sometimes it makes sense not to pursue one single career path but to adopt a shifting, growing portfolio of portable careers. Since 1987 Jo has, variously, taught word processing and other computer skills to housewives in Dubai, made and sold date chutney in Oman and taught creative writing in Norway. In The Netherlands she specialises in helping others to write their books and get published. During this time she has been involved in network marketing and sold books with Dorling Kindersley Family Learning. She has also run a CV writing service and made Christmas decorations from the flowers in her Middle Eastern garden. She is a passionate believer that flexibility and an open mind are vital attributes for anyone looking to work in another country.

In addition to the portfolio of more unusual jobs described above, Jo is primarily a writer. Her first book was published in 1985 by Octopus; a cookery book called *'French Tarts'*. She has been a journalist for seventeen years and has had hundreds of articles published all over the world in magazines such as Living Abroad, Emirates Woman, Gulf Air Golden Falcon, Expatrium, Eurograduate, Transition Abroad, Nexus, Hobson's Career Guides, Women's Business, Woman's Journal, Bonjour and Resident Abroad. She has also been published in newspapers including the Independent on Sunday, The European and The Weekly Telegraph. In addition, she runs her own publishing company, Summertime Publishing, and is perhaps best known for her *'A Career in Your Suitcase'* series. Between 1985 and 1992 she had more than 15 books published by major publishing companies. From 2000 to 2002 she was editor of Woman Abroad magazine. You can find examples of her work at:

www.expat.telegraph.co.uk

www.career–in–your–suitcase.com

www.summertimepublishing.com

www.expatica.com/hr

Foreword

Expatriates who develop entrepreneurial careers are unique and important leaders in today's increasingly global world. Their career paths and life experiences transcend the traditional, leading to extraordinary lives.

Jo Parfitt, along with her contributors, have collaborated in creating '*Expat Entrepreneurs*', which offers informative guidelines for would–be entrepreneurs abroad, as well as inspiring and powerful true–life case studies of expat entrepreneurs. These are extraordinary individuals and couples in their 20s, 30s, 40s and 50s who go abroad, usually of their own volition and make it work.

Identifying with being an entrepreneurial expat may require you to redefine your identity, rethink your definition of success, and revisit your life goals. Letting go of career perceptions and self–beliefs that no longer serve you well in order to follow the direction of your inner compass is essential for moving along your global life path. That in itself is a skill that takes time and experience to master.

Jo devotes the first section of the book to taking a closer look at the typical characteristics of a global entrepreneur. Life coaches like myself and the ones who are profiled in this book (Jacinta Noonan, Gina Teague), can help expatriate individuals, couples and entrepreneurs find ways to let go of limiting beliefs, while empowering them to developing personal and career opportunities that support their global lifestyles.

In my global life coaching practice, I see two trends emerging, supporting the idea that expatriate entrepreneurs are a growing community worldwide. First, creative and entrepreneurial folks, from musicians and writers to high–powered professionals and career changers, are moving overseas to follow a calling to pursue their careers and life dreams abroad. These entrepreneurs are often professional individuals and couples who have 5–20 years of career experience and may already be leaders in the own right. Some go abroad to 'internationalize' their life experience and career, start a new adventure or live in a place where they feel more at home.

The second trend I see is that international experience inevitably leads to personal and professional development. Short and long–term expats gain significant new insights about themselves and their place in the world while living abroad. In a foreign country people are more willing to try out new ways of doing things and being themselves, such as pursuing non–traditional and entrepreneurial work opportunities that they might not have otherwise pursued in their home countries. Couples and families may change their priorities while living abroad, most often as a result of starting a family or changing jobs or careers. They are forced to face new situations, such as how to raise multi–cultural children, how a spouse can continue a career path in a foreign country while raising a family, and how an entrepreneurial career can be the solution for life–work balance while living overseas.

By tapping into your potential as a global expat entrepreneur, you honour your true self while bringing your gifts to your local and global community. Whether you publish a cookbook, coach global clients or design websites for Internet businesses, you create a ripple effect by manifesting your potential. In this way, we all play an important role in shaping, not only our own lives abroad and those of our family members, but also the global community in which we live.

There is an increasingly accepted belief, supported by the coaching profession, that we can indeed create fulfilling lives for ourselves, wherever we choose to live in the world. Understanding your values, life priorities and global opportunities will aid you in leading an authentic life of integrity, including creating opportunities for portable global careers.

My global citizen motto is: 'Live an extraordinary life – at home and abroad'. This book opens the door of limitless possibility to become whoever you want to be, wherever you live in the world.

Elizabeth Kruempelmann

Elizabeth Kruempelmann is the founder of Global Citizen Coaching and is also a writer, wife, mother of two and a member of the American Women's Club of Düsseldorf. Her book is called '*The Global Citizen: A Guide to Creating an International Life and Career*'. She loves hearing from readers, especially global citizens, who are discovering their true paths. For more information on life coaching, see her website at www.the–global–citizen.com.

Why you should read this book

Ours is an increasingly global world. Tens of thousands of people now move overseas for work or pleasure. If this is you, read on.

International employees of multinational companies are posted, typically, for anything from a few months to several years and to a range of countries. It is not unusual for a mobile family to experience more than ten countries during an international career. If you are the spouse of an expatriate employee, and want to maintain your professional identity despite frequent upheaval, then this book is for you.

Yet, every year, thousands of families uproot themselves to move overseas for a 'better life'. Unless they can take their career with them, continue to commute or telework, these people need to find work in their adopted country. Sometime one or both partners hopes to work. Yet without locally recognised qualifications and a good command of a new language, finding paid work on the economy can be difficult or take a long time. As a result, many choose to work for themselves. If you are thinking about how to earn the bread and butter, *Brod und Boter* or *baguette et beurre,* in your new life, and would welcome some inspiration, then this book is for you too.

Even if you do not expect to work abroad, but would still like to explore some of the options open to entrepreneurs, this book remains relevant.

In short this book is for anyone who is considering working for themselves, wherever they may be, wherever they may go and whatever they may hope to become.

Contents

The Expatriate Entrepreneur

DO YOU HAVE WHAT IT TAKES?

It depends on how you look at it. Either you see an international move as the opportunity to reinvent yourself and do something new, or you see it as the end of doing something you enjoyed in a place that had become home. Of course, a move has elements of both these viewpoints, but where there are endings, there are also beginnings set to follow, and a positive attitude is vital if you want to keep your career on track.

Moving on can give you the chance to look at your personal collection of strengths, skills, talents and values and decide how you could best turn them into fulfilling work in your new location.

If you are choosing to move abroad to start a new life then the chances are you will be faced with taking your career with you, or starting a new one when you arrive. Whichever scenario seems to match your own, the move will allow you to reinvent yourself big time. Lucky you!

When Sue Burns went to Dubai, she was a nurse. While she was there she retrained as a fitness instructor and later as a swimming teacher, choosing to do work connected with her hobby, instead. Penny Tindle was a nurse too, but when she went to Norway and discovered her qualifications were not valid there she became an aromatherapist and ran ante–natal classes.

Many expatriates become inspired by the local community to branch out into a new venture that they would not otherwise have thought of back home. Sue Young switched from health centre management to running a cookery school when she moved to Paris. Her unique idea, to take expatriates first to the markets and then into school to cook the food and eat it, became 'La Toque d'Or' cookery school.

What all successful entrepreneurs have in common is a collection of traits that define them as the kind of people willing and able to run their own show, not once in one location, but repeatedly if necessary.

ARE YOU FLEXIBLE ENOUGH?

Elizabeth Kruempelmann is an American, married to a German, living in Germany. In 2003, her book, 'The Global Citizen' was published. In it she shows how a graduate can prepare for global life. Like many, Kruempelmann endorses the value of assessing your skills before you go. She provides what she calls a 'mini–course for the culturally challenged' in her book, which includes Richard Lewis's fascinating 'Lewis Model of Cultural Classification'. Do the test and discover whether you are linearactive, multiactive or reactive, then find out which cultures would best match your specific personal skills.

'Flexibility, confidence and open–mindedness are very important qualities if you want to work in Europe in a foreign culture and language,' says Kruempelmann.

It can be hard to be flexible if you have studied for a long time to work in a specific area or industry, but expatriate partners will only survive if they are willing to think laterally.

'Graduates should ask themselves whether they are willing to take a less than ideal job in an industry or company that interests them, a job where they will have the possibility of proving themselves, making contacts and moving up. This is flexibility,' continues Kruempelmann.

'They should consider whether they are able to think positively when difficult challenges come up at work, or as a result of living in a foreign culture. This is confidence.

'They should question whether they are willing to take the time to learn the language and the cultural aspects of doing business locally, instead of assuming that the way business is done at home should be the way it is done abroad. This is open–mindedness.'

CAN YOU COMMUNICATE?

Bram Lebo is the Managing Director of Expatica, a resource and network for expatriates in Northern Europe and provider of international HR news. He lives and works in Holland.

'Personal skills are your abilities to understand yourself and your colleagues and to combine that understanding with the kind of effective communication that will further both your personal and company goals,' says Lebo.

'Personal or interpersonal skills include communication skills (reading, writing letters and email), presentation skills, negotiation skills and teamwork skills. These are important because in any organisation, however small, interpersonal skills are required to send messages and directions to different parties politely and efficiently. When a person does not have interpersonal skills, he or she can be perceived as having negative characteristics such as being seen as shy, disinterested or rude. This causes friction and misunderstanding.

DO YOU UNDERSTAND?

Jeff Toms is in charge of marketing for Farnham Castle, well known for its wide range of pre–assignment preparation programmes.

'The way people do business around the world is surprisingly different. Our way of working is not necessarily valued or accepted in a different cultural environment,' explains Toms.

'People from other countries may question our professionalism in the same way that we may have doubts about their integrity. We may share similar objectives but we have different ways of achieving them. What make others tick? What do they value? How do they work and how can we work effectively with them?'

'As with anyone going to work and live in a new country it is vital to learn as much about the particular country or region as possible; history, politics, economic situation and current issues. It is equally important to learn about the business practices and social culture in order to understand why people behave the way they do. Where possible anyone relocating abroad is advised to acquire a basic grasp of the language of the country in which they will be operating, even if the working language is English.'

In addition to the skills mentioned earlier, Toms believes all expats seeking jobs should have the ability to compromise and a willingness to listen. They should also have respect for other cultures and their ways of behaving and doing things, ways that should be perceived as different rather than wrong.

Many of these skills can be learned from a book, or from the Internet; however, there is no substitute for attending a training programme, learning about a host culture and undertaking practical exercises and role–play in order to see for yourself how to create effective business and personal relationships.

ARE YOU WILLING TO LEARN?

Once overseas on assignment, the learning need never stop. Every day presents an opportunity to add to and improve your personal skills.

Once you are living local you can start thinking and acting local too, while maintaining a global perspective.

'While you are abroad you should continue to improve your skills as well as round out other global skills, such as networking and problem–solving abilities,' continues Kruempelmann.

CAN YOU WEAR THREE HATS AT ONCE?

In his best–selling books *'The E–myth'* and *'The E–myth Revisited'*, author, Michael Gerber, describes how most businesses are created out of something you already do and do well. So, for example, if you are good at making cakes, you decide to run a cake–making business; if you are good at fixing bicycles you run a bicycle–fixing business and so on. The more work you do the more you can earn. In this respect, you are what Gerber calls a *technician.* You *are* your business.

But for a business to grow you need to also be good at running the business, at keeping on top of and understanding the accounts, sales, marketing and planning of it all. To do this you need to be what Gerber calls a *manager.*

Finally, if you are to keep ahead of the competition and preserve your company's uniqueness you need to stay creative and have new ideas. Gerber calls this the *entrepreneur.*

So, do you feel comfortable being technician, manager and entrepreneur, to start with at least? It's all very well believing that you can outsource all the bits you dislike, and sure you can.

Ultimately. First of all you have to understand every aspect of your business so that you can delegate it effectively.

Being an entrepreneur is just a third of the work, you see. However, to my mind, it is the most important part. It is unlikely that an expatriate could create and maintain a career without some entrepreneurial spirit.

WHAT MAKES AN ENTREPRENEUR?

According to Iris Harvey, who co–presented a workshop on global entrepreneurship with Diane Morris at the 2002 Global Living Conference in Brussels, women–owned businesses employ more workers than the Fortune 500 companies. Women, it seems, are natural entrepreneurs.

Few people can expect a job for life, and faced with so many choices these days, few would actually want one. According to Glenda Stone, the CEO of Aurora Gender Capital Management, women move to run their own businesses because they thrive on risk. They find long–term employment poses too little of a challenge for them.

As women attempt to have it all, they are discovering that running your own business is an effective way of achieving control, flexibility, variety and challenge. It also gives them a reasonable chance of taking time off to attend the school sports day and having holidays that fit more closely round the children's needs.

Interestingly, men are increasingly attracted by the appeal of entrepreneurship too. More and more men opt to work as consultants and contractors, enjoying the buzz of change and a more flexible lifestyle.

Entrepreneurship is a key skill found in those expatriate accompanying partners who manage to create and maintain a portable career; a career that moves when they do, takes a break when they do, and can be picked up and put down again as required. Interestingly, once you have had the taste of running your own business, it can be hard to go back to routine; a set work schedule and just four weeks holiday a year.

If you think of yourself as freelance, self–employed, a sole trader or a consultant then you are an entrepreneur. Whether you make and sell strawberry jam at school craft fairs, or import goods from Vietnam into Scotland, you are still in charge of your work. You are still, effectively an entrepreneur.

When you are an entrepreneur you are in charge of:

- Investment of time
- Money
- Marketing
- Risk taking
- Innovation
- Creating the business
- Building the business

Does this sound like you?

I first went freelance in 1985, when a client I had been working for through my full–time job as a recruitment consultant, offered me the chance to write computer courses for him. I knew the job had no guarantees, and might only last six months, but I accepted. I knew that I could do some temporary secretarial work at the same time, or to tide myself over, until the next opportunity arose. I have never been employed full–time by a company since.

One of the traits of an entrepreneur is the ability to wear several hats, or juggle several different mini–careers, at once. This is commonly known as a portfolio career. I have had a portfolio of constantly shifting careers for almost 20 years now. My business streams have ebbed, flowed, and sometimes dried up completely depending on where I have been living and my other priorities at the time.

At one point, when we were living in Oman and I had two pre-school children, I spent an hour a week teaching creative writing, wrote one article a month for an airline magazine and one a month for a local publication. I also worked as a distributor for Dorling Kindersley books, holding one book party a week. Then I made date chutney and sold that to friends and at school craft fairs. In addition I would teach desktop publishing on an ad hoc basis and wrote CVs for people. None of these income streams made me a fortune, but combined they gave me my professional identity, kept my brain occupied and led me to meet new people and make new friends.

The word 'entrepreneur' is just a label. I think of myself as a serial entrepreneur, and this is typical of the expatriate accompanying partner. So let's take a look at what entrepreneurial spirit is all about.

As an entrepreneur are you:

- Confident of your abilities?
- Focused on opportunity?
- Keen to be independent?
- Able to rely on your abilities?
- Able to call on your network?
- Willing and able to grow your network?
- Happy to promote yourself and tell people what you do?
- Able to make quick decisions?
- Flexible and able to adjust to changes in opportunity and environment?
- The owner of a sense of humour?

If you can say 'yes' to any or all of the above, then you have what it takes to be an entrepreneur.

Now you know you have what it takes, you need think about the viability of your idea.

ARE YOU UP TO IT?

Before you embark on your business idea, however large or small it may be, you need to ask yourself the following questions:

- Will being an entrepreneur give me what I want from a career (money/ time off/ satisfaction/ using the skills I already have)?
- Am I happy to work sometimes long or untraditional hours?
- Does my idea use my talents and skills?
- Is my idea founded on something about which I am passionate?
- Am I good at planning and organising things?
- Am I self–motivated?
- Am I able to view mistakes as learning experiences?
- Does my family support my idea?
- Can I live with an erratic income?
- Can I afford the financial and emotional risk if this fails?
- Am I willing to under promise and over deliver?

DO YOU HAVE THE RIGHT ASSETS?

Your assets can be divided into three areas.

Firstly, *you* are your greatest asset of all. You are the sum of your skills. You are *what* you know, whether it is related to your business directly or not.

Secondly, you have another asset in all the people you know or who know you and everything and everyone they know too. At the same time, the social skills you have developed that allow you to interact and motivate other people can help you build more relationships and grow that network of resources.

Finally, you are who you *are*. You are your background and your culture. This refers to all the things you believe, and the tastes and habits you have as a result of your culture or nationality. For example, a British culture gives you the knowledge that many Brits cannot live without their Weetabix or Marmite. An American culture gives you the knowledge that Americans expect their peanut butter to come in jars striped with jam, or as they call it, *jelly*. As you travel the world you acquire more and more of this cultural expertise, some of which can be used to help you create a business. Nevertheless, cultural knowledge is not just about products, it also makes you an expert in all kinds of things that matter to that culture. Things like family values, punctuality, favourite television programmes, habits and learning styles.

Ask yourself whether you have the right personal, non–financial assets to make your idea a business success. For example, are you able to write a decent letter and keep a record of your accounts? Do you have a place, or space and time in which to work away from distractions? Do you have the equipment you need? Maybe you need a computer with certain software installed or a delivery van? Do you have the skills to use that equipment, or do you need to learn how to use it first?

Are you financially able to set up your business and run it for a while, with all the costs that entails?

Ivan Gould of Gould Associates (www.gouldassociates.co.uk) wrote the dissertation for his MBA on female entrepreneurs and believes the five traits of entrepreneurs to be:

- Desire for control

- Strong self–motivation
- Problem–solving abilities
- Flexibility and lateral thinking
- Willingness to take risk

Gould set out to try and find out whether there was any link between gender, age or marital status and the ability to be an entrepreneur. From his survey of 161 Ecademy member entrepreneurs, he discovered that that locus of control and risk–taking were pretty similar for everyone regardless of gender or situation and it was only in the other areas that differences could be seen.

DO YOU KNOW WHAT YOU WANT TO DO?

Of the above traits, one of the most important is self–motivation. If you work for yourself no–one else (apart from maybe the bank manager) is going to force you to get out of bed in the morning. And, in an exciting new country, maybe even with sunshine and the temptation of fresh coffee on the balcony, the impetus to get back inside and at a desk, can be hard to find.

The best way to ensure that you will stay motivated is to do work that you really enjoy. Better still, work that you *love*. If you do what you love it will show in your face, in your body language and in your actions. When you do something you love you will be naturally enthusiastic about your work. And that enthusiasm will become infectious. People will start to notice you and start to believe in you. In time they will start to use your services and then, when they have seen what you can do and how you put your heart and soul into your business, they will start recommending you to the people they know too. After a while all your business will come from referral. While this may sound simplistic, there is no doubt that super self–motivation leads to more money.

DO WHAT YOU LOVE

They say that when you *'do what you love the money follows'*. Marsha Sinetar wrote a book of just that title, which convinced me to follow my own heart more than 15 years ago.

So if it is so easy, why then are there also books with titles like Barbara Sher's *'I Could Do Anything I Wanted if Only I Knew What it Was*'?

I believe it is because many of us become so bogged down in the rat race, commuting and dealing with one thing after another that we forget who we are and what it is that we love to do. We do some things because we *can*, rather than because we *want to* and over time the boundary blurs between these two areas until we can no longer discern which things give us real pleasure. In his book *'The Money or Your Life'*, John Clark describes this as getting to the top of the career ladder and realising you have propped it against the wrong wall.

If you already know what it is that you want to do, then you are fortunate. But many of us remain unsure as to our true vocation. Dr Katherine Benziger is a neuro–scientist who has studied exactly this and her findings can be seen in her book *'Thriving in Mind'*. You can take her test at www.benziger.org. Benziger has discovered that when we are doing something that is our true vocation, and that we truly love, we use an unbelievable one per cent of the energy that we use when we do something else, even the things we *can* do well, or do easily. This is why, when you do something you were born to do that you can feel energised afterwards rather than drained.

It is said that we know what we love to do by the time we are nine years old. Yet, schooling, convention and other pressures force us to conform to the degree that by the time we have left school, we have no recollection of what we once wanted to do.

Yet recognising the core elements of the things we most enjoy doing can be difficult. If you are moving overseas then it is vital that you can spot which of your most transferable skills, talents and energising tasks are those that matter to you most.

There are many ways to work out who you are and therefore what will motivate you. Here are some of the most important of them:

1. **What makes you unique?**

   Discover your unique contribution. Ask yourself and others, what it is that you do both in work and your social life that really makes a difference.

2. **What matters?**

   Ask yourself what *matters* to you most in the context of work and leisure. Try not to think of subjects such as accounting or cooking but focus on things like sharing, communicating, creating or initiating.

3. **What do you need?**

   Ask yourself what you *need* to have in your work environment that you simply could not do without. Perhaps you need people around you, to get recognition, to be alone or to have a routine?

4. **What's easy?**

   Consider what it is that you do right now in work or play, that you find very easy and that makes you feel really good when you have completed it. Look for things that energise you.

5. **What have you done well?**

   Look back over your past achievements and consider what motivated you to reach those goals. Was it fame? Praise? Money? The fact that it involved being with people? A deadline maybe?

6. **What feels right?**

   Your intuition and your instinct will often tell you whether you are on the right path. Take a few days to live with each idea that you have, to imagine how life and work would be if you put it into action. Really visualise your dream. Consider how it feels in your head, your heart and your belly then follow your gut instinct.

7. **What motivates you?**

   Consider what will make you get out of bed in the morning, day after day. Think about why you think you might like to do what you are thinking about. Is it for the money alone? It shouldn't be. You should do a job because you actually *want* to. The work itself must motivate you. Or do you want to do it for the recognition, the satisfaction, because it will keep you busy, let you meet people? Be honest here.

Start doing some soul–searching. It is vital that you research your own desires and motivations before you decide on a new career overseas. Overseas you will be alone and without the support network of friends and colleagues that you have become used to back home.

I would recommend reading some books such as those mentioned above, and scheduling yourself plenty of thinking time. If you can, hire a career coach or work with a careers consultant. A coach will be able to guide you through all the processes I have mentioned before and many more.

But if you do nothing else make a promise to yourself that you will start asking people who know you well as a person and as a colleague what they consider to be your strengths and weaknesses. You may be in for some surprises.

If you want to learn more about how to find your passion then take a look at my book, *'Find Your Passion'*, available from www.bookshaker.com

CREATE YOUR IDEA

If you are lucky then the job you take with you can be exactly the same as the one you left behind. You pack up your tools of the trade and you are ready to work when you arrive. However, it is not always that simple. A plumber, for example, may need to make sure his or her qualifications are recognised in the destination country and to join the relevant members' associations before he is legally entitled to trade.

While nursing appears at first glance to be wholly portable as every country needs nurses, it is not always straightforward. For example, in Norway, a nurse can only be employed in the national health service if his or her Norwegian is fluent. And though an aromatherapist or reflexologist can trade in England after taking a short course, in Germany a complementary therapist must also be a qualified nurse. Language and qualifications are stumbling blocks that must be considered.

CAN YOU TAKE YOUR CLIENTS?

And if you do think you can take your current business with you, will your clients come too? Though trades like car mechanics, building and gardening may be easily transferred to a foreign location, do not under–estimate how long it will take you to establish your business and get clients. If you need physical customers to come through your door then expect it to take a year or two to build your business to a reasonable level. If you work online, and your clients are 'virtual', then there is no reason why you can't take them with you.

People do business with people they like and who are like them. Networking is the key to meeting people with whom you can create first a social and then a commercial connection.

DO YOU HAVE AN EYE FOR A MARKET?

And what of your market? Do you know that people will want what you have to offer in your new location? Can you prove it? Sometimes what works well in one place fails in another even though the business is a great idea. This is when you may have to think laterally, and consider how to alter your business to fit the market and the climate.

When Paul and Julia Herbert landed in France a decade ago, they had no idea what they were going to do and started off by helping local part–time expatriate residents to rent out their villas to holidaymakers. Their talent for spotting opportunities and building a talented network so that they can go for them has led to them now running more than 100 websites, all linked to the holiday business. Find them at www.whereonearthgroup.com

HOW PORTABLE IS YOUR CAREER?

Take a moment to assess the tools of your trade and consider how portable they may be.

The following may weigh nothing, but can you really take them with you:

- Education
- Experience

- Qualifications ... check they are recognised overseas
- Language skills ... check the level of fluency required
- Database of clients
- Network and networking skills
- Market and marketing skills
- Business experience
- Ability to think laterally
- Information sources

Being an entrepreneur means that you are able to think outside the box. You may have an idea for a product that would be perfect for one specific market; an entrepreneur will take that idea further. Think about other products that may appeal to that same market, or other markets that may find that same product attractive. Consider how you might manage to sell additional products at the same time, or how to tempt existing clients to spend more money. These two areas are called cross–selling and up–selling.

When you have your idea, think about whether you want it to stay where it is, or whether you could have plans for expansion.

CREATE THE VENTURE

In some countries, starting a business is as simple as opening a bank account and informing the tax office of your plans. In others you may need to find a local partner or sponsor before you can create your business.

Consider whether you want to be solely responsible for your business, or whether you would prefer to work in a team. If marketing or sales is not your forté, then maybe you could team up with someone else who does that, while you concentrate on creating products or delivering your service?

If there are any areas of business that you know you need, but do not have the skills for, consider whether you know other people who could help. Maybe you need someone to mind the children for you so you can have some time in your office, or maybe you need someone to teach you how to desktop publish your own marketing materials. As long as you know someone you can hire, or exchange skills with, you can consider that area covered.

If you work with a partner or two you could find a way to share projects, contacts, research or other information. Maybe you could share resources, investment or equipment? Perhaps one of you could provide an office while another provides a computer or the use of a vehicle? If you would prefer something more informal, then maybe you could hook up with someone who wants to run a completely different venture from yours, but with whom you could exchange services. Maybe you could write the marketing material if she designs it, for example.

When Sue Valentine was in Oman, she got the British Council to employ her as an *ad hoc* consultant, which meant they paid her no salary but did provide her with a work permit. All the freelance consultancy work she undertook was invoiced via this sponsor.

When Anne Love wanted to write a gardening book, she helped people with their gardens in exchange for help with photographs and design.

Sometimes it is feasible for you to collaborate with someone in another country. For example, you could be employed by a French company, and therefore paid in France, while you work for them in a different country.

To summarise: you could go it alone, collaborate with local expatriates, with local nationals or with an overseas organisation.

Think about what would work for you and fit with your goals before formalising anything.

Check you understand and comply with all the legal considerations of your business before you start.

MARKET YOUR IDEA

It has been discovered that successful entrepreneurs consider the following when marketing their businesses:

- They start with an idea and THEN try to find a market for it
- They are excited about new ideas and concepts
- They anticipate and adapt to new trends and opportunities
- They start small
- They grow slowly
- They test the market and new ideas carefully before rolling them out
- They use their intuition
- They are great networkers
- They obtain most of their business through word of mouth and referrals
- They are not afraid to ask for what they want

It does not matter how good your product is, if you have no market for it. Think about who will buy your product or service.

- Will you sell to businesses, individuals or organisations?
- How will you target that market?
- Could you give talks about your area of expertise to local clubs?
- Could you write articles on the subject for the local press?
- Could you create a flyer and post it through letterboxes, or make a poster for a school, supermarket or library notice–board?

- Can you afford to advertise in the paper or on the radio, or would a short piece about you in the school magazine be just as effective?
- Which networking groups could you join in order to meet potential clients?
- If there is no suitable network for you to join, would you start your own?
- If you plan to start a website, will you send out a regular newsletter or e–zine to keep yourself and your business in the minds of the subscribers?

Iris Harvey, whom I mentioned earlier, has reinvented herself several times as she has moved internationally. She now has Mitsubishi and Prudential among the clients for her company, which she calls Marketing Strategies and Solutions. Iris suggested all entrepreneurs do the following three things:

- Learn to distil your business message into two or three clever sentences, in order to make an impact quickly and effectively.
- Prepare a list of all the local and other relevant media (magazines, radio, TV, websites) who might be interested in writing about what you do.
- Prepare a press kit that explains what you do, together with any clippings or testimonials, ready to send to anyone who shows an interest.

WHY NETWORKING WORKS

I am a firm believer in networking. As you read through the case studies that follow keep a look out for the ingenious ways these entrepreneurs have found new clients.

Networking is a simple and as natural as making friends. As I said earlier, we do business with people who are like us. What's more we do business with people who like us. We are more likely to give a job to someone we know, simply because we know them, than we are to someone we don't know whose work may be of a higher quality or cheaper. You can never have too many friends.

Interestingly, most referral business comes to us indirectly via our 'friends' rather than from the friends themselves. So, don't worry about where or whom you are meeting too much, they will still help you grow your business. For example, you may be about to start a meat importing business and then you play against someone at the tennis club who is a vegetarian. It is not wise to discount the potential of your new partner, for she may have plenty of friends who are carnivores, or be the sister–in–law of a man who runs the most successful steak house in town.

Good networkers do not give out business cards and brochures. Instead they give out what I call 'presents'. Gifts that cost nothing. Good networkers are always on the look out to see what they can do for other people, how they can help, and how they can connect them. So, if you meet someone who is looking for a local dentist and you are happy with your own, tell the person you have just met about yours and give her the phone number. The best gifts of all cost you nothing but make a big difference to the recipient. The best networkers are generous of spirit.

The more you can give to others the more you will receive in return. Networking is a bit like throwing boomerangs. You send out your gift like a boomerang and have no idea where it will land or how it will come back to you. But it *will* come back and often from the most unusual direction. The unwritten law of the boomerang though, is that the more you dive, duck and dash to try and intercept it, the more unlikely it is to go in the opposite direction. So relax and trust the law of karma and believe me, you will receive.

The most effective networking you can do is to join a club or group, a sports club or professional networking group. Then when you are a member start being an *active* member. Offer to help out, to welcome newcomers or assist with fundraisers. The more visible you can be the better. Then, offer to be on the board. The higher your profile the more generous you will appear and the more people are likely to appreciate and get to like you. Now you are visible every member and guest of the group will get to know you, and before long your client base will grow to reflect this.

Like tending a garden, good networking is all about tending, nurturing and paying attention. But, like gardening, you also need to prune and trim back the networks that truly do not work for you either personally or professionally.

If you want to learn more about networking then take a look my book, '*Grow Your Own Networks*', available from www.bookshaker.com

Local networking will help your business locally of course, but if you run a global business either over the Internet, or you want clients who are further afield, then virtual networks are invaluable. Ecademy is a terrific international group that helps people to connect worldwide over the Internet, but it also has many live groups too. Again, join discussion groups, contribute to forums and help to answer questions for other people. Your generosity and willingness to join in will pay dividends.

GETTING STARTED

However small your business is, you need to start out with a number of marketing tools, contacts and advice. These should ideally include:

- A corporate identity or brand with a logo and slogan
- Business cards and letterhead
- An e–mail address
- A website
- A telephone with answering machine
- A postal address
- A computer with email and word processing software
- Membership of professional or trade associations
- Networking expenses
- An outfit to wear that perpetuates your brand
- Legal advice
- Accounting and tax advice
- A place and time to work without interruption

GETTING INSPIRATION FOR YOUR OWN BUSINESS

One of the best ways to come up with a great business idea is to talk to people, and, importantly, to listen to what they say. Listen to what people are complaining about and you have the opportunity to create a business that will provide a solution. If people moan that they see too little sun, open a tanning parlour. If they moan about how much they miss a type of pickle, start making and selling your own. It was when Sue Valentine and I were involved in a conversation in which one of our friends remarked how she had no idea how to cook dates, that Sue and I decided to write a cookery book, called '*Dates*'.

If you listen, you can turn other people's problems into your opportunity.

Make time to brainstorm. Meet with a group of friends or acquaintances who would all benefit from some time discussing their business ideas or problems and take it in turns to brainstorm with each other. I call these sessions 'blue sky' parties.

Go on a course, mix with people you find inspiring or creative and soon you will be inspired too.

Or, of course, you can buy yourself a few books. My own book, '*A Career in Your Suitcase*', is well known for inspiring people to get cracking on their new career. You can purchase it at www.bookshaker.com. And there are plenty of other good books and websites out there. The site www.fabjob.com sells a range of affordable e–books that help you get started on a new career. Simply browsing the list of titles on offer is inspiring.

Simon Kent is the author of *Odd Jobs*, published by Kogan Page. He describes a range of interesting, unorthodox careers that frequently come about as a result of a chance remark, coincidence or new friendship. The opening line of the book is 'Warning! This is not a careers book.' And, while it contains a wide range of options, it does not pretend to be a substitute for doing your own research.

Kent's book is designed to inspire people to search off the beaten track for jobs they quite fancy doing rather than delivering a clear career structure in any particular field.

'This is largely through necessity. There is no single way to become a club DJ, pyrotechnics specialist or performance artist, for example,' he continues. 'I guess a bungee jumper could find a UK based bungee jumping company and see if they're operating in the country of destination and will take them on, but this seems an outside chance. My top tip in terms of odd jobs would therefore be to go to the country and see what the possibilities are. Find out if there are activities taking place which a trailing partner enjoys and can get involved in.'

If you fancy finding out more about careers in, say, the manufacture of fresh cosmetics, body piercing, paint balling, driving a rickshaw or being a taxidermist, then 'Odd Jobs' will fascinate you. Each job description includes suggestions of the highs and lows you may encounter, and continues with a useful list of facts, links and trivia resources.

'On average British job tenure is now 5.32 years. 60 per cent of UK interviewees in a recent survey have completely changed careers at least once . . . 20 per cent said they would choose to do something completely different,' say Stuart Crainer, Stephen Coomber and Des Dearlove, the authors of another new career book. '*The Career Adventurer's Fieldbook*', which is appropriately jacketed in combat colours, is published by Wiley.

While this book does not go into the same detail about unusual career options, as Kent's publication, it provides, instead, a range of case studies as well as a new spin on the way to look at your career path. In the chapter entitled 'The Road Less Travelled', the authors discuss the rise of the entrepreneur and through a series of tasks, they call 'adventures', help you to decide whether you are ready for the journey. There are many case studies and comments from people who have experienced it all. From people working as a chocolate tester for Safeway to being a professional speaker, animal behaviourist or playing a Japanese drum called a Taiko.

'A career is no longer a hard slog through the ranks of a single organisation. It is a series of adventures: a journey towards enlightenment. It is a search for the perfect fit between you and your work,' say the authors.

The Career Adventurer's Fieldbook is not just designed to inspire you. It is crammed with tools and insights into surviving the jungle that is the world of work. From preparing your CV, to retirement it has solid advice and facts about vital topics such as networking, surviving redundancy, mentoring and burn out.

If you want to turn the problem of constant moving into an opportunity, consider taking a leaf out of the books of the people and the authors mentioned above, and do something different this time.

ARE YOU READY?

If the previous pages have tempted you to have a go at being an entrepreneur and creating your own fully portable, tailor made career, then you will find more inspiration in the rest of this book.

What follows is a selection of case studies of trailblazer men and women who have developed their entrepreneurial spirit while living overseas as expatriates. They have worked in a range of countries and for a range of industries. Read their stories, find out how they did it, and pick up tips on how you can do it too.

Good luck.

Jo Parfitt

PS If you would like to receive a monthly dose of inspiration, please go to my website www.career–in–your–suitcase.com and sign up for my free e–zine, called The Inspirer. It is always my pleasure to help other people to find their perfect, portable career.

PPS If you find your own perfect portable career, or know someone else who would be suitable for the next edition of Expatriate Entrepreneurs, please get in touch with me at jo@summertimepublishing.com

Expat Entrepreneurs

BETH HOUGH–KOESTAL

Key Information
Artist, Teacher, Entrepreneur, Pioneer, Professional, Marketer, Adviser and Art Historian
Age: Fiftyish
Nationality: American
Status: Married
Countries lived in: USA, The Netherlands, Republic of Germany, Belgium
Qualifications: Degree in Fine Art, Art Education, post graduate studies under well–known master painters in genre of classical realism. Member of Portrait Society of America, Belgian Watercolor Society and Professional Picture Framers Association. Second Language Skills: Dutch (university level diploma), German, French
Years on the move: 20

Teresa Beth Hough–Koestal is so many things – all of them rolled into one intense, energised, and positive human being. A gifted artist, specialising in portraits and landscapes, Beth is driven primarily by her benevolent desire to share her knowledge and understanding of art with all who are willing to learn.

Beth grew up in a small North Carolina community near Charlotte and developed her artistic interests at the University of North Carolina where she received a Bachelor's degree in art education as well as a Master of Fine Arts degree. Her career path has led her from rural North Carolina to Waterloo, Belgium where the sum of her education and experience has culminated in a thriving career as an artist, instructor, and entrepreneur.

After graduating from college, Beth earned her living back in her home community with private commissions of portraits and homes. She eventually opened her own frame shop and gallery. In 1984, Beth moved to New York with the intention of developing her artistic interests, but instead landed a job with a Fortune 500 company on Wall Street. Beth not only demonstrated success as a sales–person, but she also met her husband, Jaap Koestal, a native of Amsterdam.

Beth moved with her husband to Europe in 1988, residing first in Amsterdam, then Düsseldorf, and finally in Waterloo, which is 18 kilometres south of Brussels. In Waterloo, Beth has not only discovered her life's work, but she has found a beautiful, inspiring setting for her artistic endeavours. Waterloo serves as an excellent launching point for the art workshops she runs in Provence, Paris and Normandy, which trace the very paths and places frequented by Monet, Cézanne, and Van Gogh.

Beth offers a wide array of art education options for all ages. She firmly believes that learning art will not only develop the more creative areas of the brain, but will enable the students to understand and appreciate what they see in new and improved ways. She insists that artistic talent is not necessarily a divine gift, but rather a skill that can be learned and developed with the right teacher and the right kind of instruction.

'Anyone who has the desire, and makes a conscious decision to learn, can. From there, it's more a matter of following a few well–explained steps,' said Hough–Koestal. 'Once you understand the fundamentals – drawing skills and composition – you can adapt these skills into any medium, whether watercolour, oil painting or anything else.'

Beth approaches her students with what she describes as a 'relaxed attitude' towards drawing, and injects her sense of fun and humour into all her efforts. She divides her students into three practice levels: beginning, improving, or perfecting skills and offers workshops in her Waterloo studio and abroad, as mentioned earlier. Tuition for the courses ranges from minimal fees to $1,500.

One of her more popular courses is her 'Classical Provence Workshop Abroad', which is held in spring each year for students of all levels. The one–week course begins in Avignon, France, where Beth meets the students and chauffeurs them to their residence for the week; a 300–year–old flourmill converted into attractive and comfortable apartments. A specialist chef, formerly featured on French television is brought in to prepare gourmet and customised meals including picnics for *plein air* sessions. Beth leads the group on daily excursions throughout southern France to draw, paint and practise various artistic techniques in the shadow of famous artists.

In 2002 Beth launched a new workshop entitled, 'The Monet Route to Normandy'. This tour through Normandy features *en plein air* (outdoor) painting in villages and areas known to Monet. In addition, Beth has developed a mini–college curriculum that provides a logical sequence of courses designed especially for American expatriates who are located in Europe for one to three years.

'This gives them a tangible, marketable skill that they can develop while they are in Europe and then take home and continue to develop,' said Hough–Koestal.

Other art courses offered throughout the year from her Waterloo studio include 'Drawing for those who can't (absolute beginners)' 'Discovery Stream, one day workshops in various media', and 'Kids Art Camp' (summer) and Art Attic (after school). Beth adores teaching.

'I teach because I enjoy being around people and like the idea of not really getting away from art. Previously, when I painted I wondered what I was missing and if I socialised I often had the guilt of not being at the easel. Then, one day, quite by accident, I met with a fellow volunteer in my home for some charity work. At a particular point, she noticed an oversized pencil drawing on the wall and began to gush compliments. Because it was an older work and signed in my maiden name, she was not aware she was talking about my work. Of course, I gladly confessed and her final comment was just as enthusiastic and proved to be life–changing, 'If you ever teach, I want to be in your class!'

'This became the perfect answer – luckily there were others who felt the same way. Now I offer a series of classes throughout the year, but average only one day a week teaching. In this way I socialise and sharpen my skills at the same time' she says. 'It is very rewarding to see displaced people develop talents they were unsure existed and meet new friends. I know time spent with art offers balance for many people in other ways. Developing one's artistic side lets the individual see everything more acutely. Common experiences like selections for getting dressed each day, setting a table, viewing art are all heightened. It's wonderful to see this change take place.'

Beth continues to market her own work, which can be viewed in homes and galleries throughout the United States and Europe. She accepts both private and corporate commissions and periodically makes presentations and demonstrations to audiences of fellow artists, such as the lecture on portraiture and demonstration in watercolour for the Portrait Society of Canada in Ottawa.

In addition to her artistic pursuits, Beth and her husband, Jaap, are also developing their hobby of collecting 18th and 19th Century English, French and Dutch furniture and accessories into a new business, which will eventually have both European and US locations. Along with an impressive inventory, 'Dutch and Duchess' already have some unique courses up and running. One of their most popular courses takes place on a one–day bus trip to the antique markets of Paris. Want to find out how to tie a scarf in more than sixty different ways? No problem. That's another one–day trip to a factory outlet practising Beth's tips with the help of her book. Both courses are actually taught on the bus, en–route to the destination. With Beth's artistic eye and a Dutchman's flair for recognising value and quality, this hobby could develop into another success story.

Beth is not only a gifted artist and teacher, but she is also a courageous pioneer who has carved out a niche for herself and other women in pursuit of opportunities abroad. In a land that inspired Monet and Van Gogh amongst others to paint masterpieces, Beth has chosen to share her knowledge and passion for art with all who care to collect art or develop their creative inclinations.

BETH WOULD LIKE TO SHARE THE FOLLOWING

You can contact Beth on: kunstkrant@tiscali.be

Website: www.dutchnduchess.com

Magazines

International Artist: www.artinthemaking.com

Has international offices, thus requires no extra postage or subscriptions. It has competitions in each issue, excellent technical explanations, often in two–page spreads.

The Pastel Journal: www.pasteljournal.com

Taken over in 2003 by The Artist magazine, targets advanced artists, so the learning curve for beginners is very steep. NB Pastels are the fastest growing medium in fine arts and the purest medium available for artists.

Books

Edwards, B *The New Drawing on the Right side of the Brain*, HarperCollins

Goldfinger, *Human Anatomy for Artists*, Oxford University Press

Brookes, M *Drawing for Older Children and Teens: A Creative Method for Adult Beginners Too*, Tarcher

Diamond, M and Hopson, J *Intelligence, Creativity, and Healthy Emotions from Birth Through Adolescence*, Plume Books

Organisations

Portrait Society of America: www.portraitsociety.org

American Society of Portrait Artists: www.portraitartist.com

Shaw Guides for Artists: www.shawguides.com

Beth's Tips

Join a club: Join the local Community Artist Organisations or start one if that doesn't exist. It is easy to start one, compose an ad as if the organization already exists with a specific meeting date and initially put yourself as the contact.

Invite other artists: Invite notable artists to demonstrate at meetings.

Have an exhibition: Organise a judged exhibition once a year or form a group to open up your studios during the holidays.

GINA TEAGUE

Key Information

A Career in Cross–Cultural Training

Age: 45

Nationality: British

Status: Married

Countries lived in: France, Spain, Brazil, US, Australia

Qualifications: BA Modern Languages, MA Organisational Psychology, EdM Counselling Psychology

Years on the move: 23

Gina Teague found herself on the expatriate circuit shortly after leaving university with a degree in Modern Languages. Having spent a semester in Madrid, Gina decided to return and pursue a career in Teaching English as a Second Language (TESOL). Later she moved to Brazil where she met and married her husband and has now been living abroad for over 20 years.

Married to an Australian, with two 'Third Culture Kids', Jack and Caroline, Gina has experienced the gamut of expatriate issues. Although she has lived in the USA for the majority of the time, Gina has also lived in France, Spain and Brazil and has recently moved to Sydney, Australia.

Her expatriate lifestyle has led her into a career that has focused largely on cross–cultural training and careers counselling. She now has an MA in Organisational Psychology and an MEd in Counselling Psychology to her credit.

'I stumbled upon the world of cross–cultural training, really,' explains Gina. 'It all began when I took an elective class in the subject while doing my first Master's. As part of the assignment I had to interview someone active in the field. I chose to speak to an interculturalist and we ended up talking about my experiences in Brazil. Two years later, out of the blue, she called to ask me if I would like to consider working in this field.' Gina's first brief was to help a single, professional woman from London settle in New York. The actual work this entailed ranged from analysis of cross–cultural business practices to waiting for her cable guy to arrive.

It is Gina's personal experience of living and working abroad that have been the catalyst for her career. There is no such thing as a typical cross–cultural training regime, as Gina explains:

'For each type of work, the process is slightly different. However, as a rule, most of my work involves an extensive needs assessment, custom designing a training programme, coaching or counselling session, delivery and follow–up. As an independent contractor, I also invest a lot of time in researching local market needs, and engaging in professional development courses and attending conferences to stay abreast of new research and trends.'

'The fact that I have lived the expat life gives me a level of practical knowledge and empathy with clients who are about to embark on an overseas assignment. I've covered pretty much the entire expat spectrum; I have lived overseas as a student, single professional, married professional, married trailing–spouse–with–no–work–visa, parent of Third Culture Kids and now in my current incarnation of expat with portable career.'

For a person who thrives on challenge and variety, working in cross–cultural training affords ample helpings of both. There are days when Gina spends hours working from home 'in sweatpants' doing research and program design. Then there are days when she has to put on a suit and deliver a counselling session or group programme in a corporate environment. The money isn't bad either. Although there is a wide range of pay for cross–cultural training, in the US it is common for trainers to earn between $500 and $1,000 for a one–day program. Gina supplements her training and counselling with additional writing and consultancy projects. But perhaps what makes her chosen career of particular interest to others looking for a mobile career is that it can be conducted from a home office, anywhere in the world.

Like any professional expatriate partner, Gina cites the lack of stability and the need to re–establish her business with each new posting as the worst aspects of her work. But this is a trade off against the variety, autonomy and ultimate portability of her career. Gina advises others who may be interested in a similar career to research the area thoroughly beforehand.

'Try to read the 'gurus' of the field, and conduct information interviews,' she advises and recommends that you ascertain which areas of the field are most in demand in your host country.

'It can be helpful to engage in a self–assessment process,' she suggests. 'Undertake a series of exercises to help pinpoint your career related values, interests and skills to find out which chosen field might be a good fit. Primarily I work with corporate expats and their spouses and families. Much of my work centres around the spouse's personal and professional development plans. However, in addition to my work in relocation, I also do work in the domestic career development arena, as well as in the intercultural field.

If you think that cross–cultural training is for you, then seriously consider taking a 'Train the Trainers' course, such as that provided by Dr Anne Copeland of the Interchange Institute. Many companies require a Master's degree too. Attend conferences and join professional associations. Finally, and most importantly, talk to current and former expats and read books or articles on the subject who will have blazed the trail for you.'

Cross–cultural training does carry with it a large amount of responsibility. You are the main source of support and information for somebody who is about to embark on what will probably be a major life (and career) transition. You must be meticulously prepared and be ready to give every counselling and coaching session 110%.

Networking provided Gina with her first job in this field and continues to be the source of 95 per cent of her work.

'Although my new business, *World of Difference: Cultural & Career Services* does have a website and full range of marketing materials, I find that the majority of 'leads' come from networking, from referrals, recommendations and from being visible in professional associations and conferences.'

The importance of maintaining global contacts whilst also developing local ones cannot be over–emphasised. While the founding of *World of Difference* reflected the need to establish a presence in the local marketplace, Gina remains an active partner in *Isis Group International,* the cross–cultural consultancy that she co–founded in the US with fellow interculturalists Sonja Schlegel–Breemen and Catherine Tansey.

'This is truly the best of both worlds: *World of Difference* gives local clients the confidence that I can offer targeted information in terms of Australian relocation and job search issues, while *Isis* offers an international presence – and the support and synergy of being associated with 2 of America's premier interculturalists.'

In 2003 Gina was commissioned to write a book on living in America for the CultureSmart series. *'Culture Smart USA'* was published in July 2004 by Kuperard, UK and showed that Gina had settled in to a new country well enough to be regarded as an authority on the subject. She had, herself, become a 'guru'.

GINA WOULD LIKE TO SHARE THE FOLLOWING

You can contact Gina on:

gina@worldofdifference.com.au

info@worldofdifference.com.au

For books by the 'gurus' such as Trompenaars, Hofstede and Hampden–Turner please look at:

www.interculturalpress.com

www.nbrealey–books.com

In addition to undergraduate and graduate programmes, in the US training courses for would be cross–cultural trainers are provided by Jeremy Solomons (Jersol@aol.com) and Dr Anne Copeland (copeland@interchangeinstitute.org)

Consider taking a course run by the Summer Intercultural Institute. For more information contact Barbara Schaetti at: www.transitiondynamics.com

Conferences

Families in Global Transition Conference: www.figt.org

SIETAR (Society for Intercultural Education, Training & Research: www.sietarusa.org

Gina's Tips

Be a generous networker: What goes around comes around! Be sensitive to the unwritten rules of networking (especially respecting people's time) – and also differences in the acceptability of certain networking approaches across cultures.

Get noticed: Raise your profile by writing, presenting, attending conferences, volunteering for committees, and generally 'being a player' in your particular field.

Specialise AND diversify: It's important to develop a niche – a specialised area of expertise that you become associated with. However, you should also focus on developing new skills and expanding your knowledge in areas that complement your core field of expertise.

KRISTIN ENGVIG

Key Information

Founder and organiser of the Women's International Networking (WIN) conference

Age: 38

Nationality: Norwegian

Status: Partner, with one child

Countries lived in: Norway, Australia, Japan, Switzerland, Italy

Qualifications: Degree in Business Administration and Marketing, Oslo School of Business; MBA, Bocconi University Business School, Milan. Numerous courses in Acting

Years on the move: 17

Kristin became founder and director of WIN conferences in 1998 after working for five years as an international consultant and specialist on intercultural management issues and marketing/communication strategies. Prior to becoming a consultant, Kristin pursued an active career in international companies such as Citibank and JP Morgan, and was responsible for public relations for the Norwegian Export Council in Japan. As a consultant she has worked in Western and Eastern Europe in particular Bulgaria, Lativia, Lituania and Russia., is passionate about acting and yoga and speaks five languages.

Kristin is now producing the ninth annual WIN conference, which was held in Milan for four years and Lausanne for two and Geneva for two. To date more than 50 international women's networks endorse the WIN conference and several thousand women have asked to be added to their mailing list connecting women worldwide.

Having lived abroad for 17 years Kristin is passionate about the value of networking. Subsequent to two years as President of the Professional Women's Association, Milan, combined with European travel as a consultant, she recognised an increasing need for an event that would make it easier for women to work internationally. In September 1998 the first WIN conference took place.

'The conference is a catalyst that now has a track record of being one of the most powerful networking events of the year,' explains Kristin. 'But it is also committed to helping women prepare for change, discover opportunities and identify their personal strengths.

'I felt the need to do something that facilitated the difficult situation for women working internationally. I knew that we could all learn from the inspiration and experiences of others.'

Yet Kristin believes that in our quest we should stay women, not strive to be men, but stay true to ourselves.

'It can be so easy for a capable and secure woman to feel both misplaced and insecure in a foreign country. WIN' s objective is to ensure that all conference participants go home stronger, more confident and more committed than ever to creating or maintaining sustainable ventures, even internationally,' she continues.

WIN is run by a dedicated multinational team of volunteers and professionals who, with Kristin at the helm, spend at least six months producing a conference, despite limited resources, that is bigger and better than the year before. Sponsors are needed, and are forthcoming, with P&G, The Dow Chemical Company, IBM, HP, Whirlpool and the International Herald Tribune being regular supporters.

Each year conference numbers increase markedly and in 2005 they welcomed 500 participants from 58 countries. Feedback is always complimentary and positive, with an overall rating of 98 per cent, and many attendees have said it was 'the best conference they have ever attended.'

Kristin has always been motivated by her dreams and has been determined to put her ideas into action. WIN 98 was just an experiment, but after four years in Italy and now another four in Switzerland she has encouraged other cities to hold the event. Ultimately Kristin would like to see WIN events in other world capitals, even beyond Europe.

She is now writing a book on WIN, the many concepts it has developed and the amazing international women who have been part of its success.

'I believe in many things,' she says. 'It is important to focus, prioritise, find quality in your life, look after your health and strive to invent rather than copy. If women work in collaboration we can lead real world change.

In 2001 Kristin became a mother to a little boy called Leonardo and since then she has cut down her consulting work considerably, choosing instead to focus on the conferences. She believes that all women, whether or not they are mothers, have a unique opportunity in that they are able to use their female qualities in order to build sustainable environments for future generations.

KRISTIN WOULD LIKE TO SHARE THE FOLLOWING

You can contact Kristin on: Kristinengvig@winconference.net

Kristin Engvig
Founder and Director WIN
Leadership Events for Women Working Internationally
CBC–L, Rue de Simplon 37,
1006 Lausanne,
CH
Tel:00 41 216120355
www.winconference.net

Books

Rubin, H *The Princessa: Machiavelli for Women*, Doubleday

Stassinopoulos, A *Conversations with the Goddesses,* Stewart, Tabori & Chang

Eisler, R *The Power of Partnership: Seven Relationships that will Change Your Life*, New World Library

Senge,P *The Fifth Discipline Fieldbook: Strategies for Building a Learning Organisation*, Nicholas Brealey Publishing

Cameron, J *The Artist's Way*, Tarcher

Williamson, M *A Return to Love*, HarperCollins

Kristin's Tips

Never copy: innovate

Live creatively

Never give up

Have fun

Make sure you light people up and feel lighted up as often as possible yourself

EMMA BIRD

Key Information

A career as a writer, teacher and Italy expert

Age: 29

Nationality: British

Status: Living with Sardinian boyfriend

Countries lived in: France, Corsica, Italy, Sardinia

Qualifications: CELTA TEFL qualification, BA European Studies in French and Italian, Post–graduate Diploma in Newspaper Journalism

Years on the move: 10

Emma Bird was bitten by the travel bug when she was just 19 and went to work as an au pair in Naples. She loved it so much that when she was 20 she returned there to complete the third year of her degree in Bologna before returning to the UK to complete her fourth and final year of study.

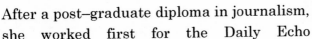

After a post–graduate diploma in journalism, she worked first for the Daily Echo Bournemouth (where in fact she had also done work between the ages of 15 and 21) as a Junior Reporter before she went to work for the Liverpool Daily Post, becoming a Senior Reporter. Aged just 24, she promised to buy herself an inspiring book that would motivate her and bought a copy of *'Buying a Home in Italy'* by David Hampshire. Shortly afterwards, on her 25th birthday she resigned and two months later, in early 2002, she was in Milan working as the Italian correspondent for World Textile Publications. This time she was abroad for keeps.

Yet the job was demanding, Emma found the writing dissatisfying and she had no time left to explore the country. She left after six months.

'I had had no time to network and so I had no local contacts at this point,' recalls Emma. 'But I wanted to stay in the city so I headed back to my home town of Bournemouth and studied at the International Teaching and Training Centre where a month intensive teacher training course cost just over £1,000. In January 2003 I began work in a language school back in Milan.'

The school paid €10 an hour, while private lessons paid three times that. It was impossible for Emma to stay in her studio flat in a smart part of Milan and so moved to share a company flat with colleagues and taught like crazy in order to earn a decent wage.

In late 2002 Emma met a Sardinian called Mario, who was working for a big fashion IT holding. Then in May 2003 she moved with him to Sardinia, an island of just 1.6M inhabitants and very few expatriates. Despite being a natural networker, Emma felt like a fish out of water.

'Coming to Sardinia was the classic culture shock experience. I didn't identify with anyone and there were no expatriate clubs or networking groups. By the summer I was too lethargic and depressed to create my own group,' she recalls.

'Then in December, I was reminded that I was the kind of person to grab every opportunity going and create my own too. I decided that I would set up two groups, one for expatriates and one for women who wanted to network professionally.'

Emma kept herself busy teaching English, but it was not long before the idea of running a network became a reality and Weaveaweb was born.

'I took my inspiration for Weaveweb from existing virtual and real–time groups like TalentedWomen (www.talentedwomen.com), Ecademy (www.ecademy.com) and the Professional Women's Association (www.pwa–milan.org), which has an active group in Milan,' she says.

As a result Emma created two companion websites: Weaveaweb, which promotes networks and networking events all over first Sardinia, and now an increasing amount of Italy, and HowtoItaly, which is for current and potential expatriates to the country. HowtoItaly is a consulting company helping current and potential expats realise their dream of living and working in Italy successfully. The Weaveaweb site is in English and Italian and designed for both foreign and Italian women who speak Italian and who work as freelancers or run their own businesses. It also lists workshops, social events, job opportunities, books and has a wide range of related content.

Real–time groups now meet once a month for dinner, lunch or a drink in a variety of cities. The group focuses particularly on women who are freelance and small business owners, though it is gaining in popularity with other professionals too.

'Italians are still very new to the idea of networking and charging people to come to events would not happen, especially in the smaller towns,' says Emma, who has ambitions to grow the group still further and hold more, fee–paying events in time.

Then, in 2005, Emma started sending out monthly ezines from her sites. The Howtoitaly magazine now has more than 1,500 subscribers and is in English and the Weaveaweb one, which goes to more than 700 people now, is in Italian. She uses the newsletter creation and management company called ConstantContact (www.constantcontact.com) for the database and autoresponders and then Wiredeyes (www.wiredeyes.com) for the design.

The next venture is a conference for Italian–speaking women and will be held in Cagliari, in Sardinia in 2006.

'Sardinia is cut off from Italy not only geographically but also in terms of services. There are few training courses on the island, which means there are few opportunities for professional and personal growth. I decided there was a need to bring courses to Sardinia and so am planning a weekend of networking and seminars to inspire and inform.'

The conference is being jointly organised by Valeria Pintus, marketing manager of Cybervision (www.cybervision.it), who is Sardinian and has lived and worked in London.

It wasn't long before Emma was writing again too.

'You can take the girl out of newspaper journalism, but you can't take the newspaper journalism out of the girl,' she says. 'I always carry a notebook with me, even a teeny weeny one, with an even teenier pen, if I'm out for the evening and that I can cram into a purse the size of a credit card. I am always on the look out for ideas and potential stories. Many articles are based on something that happens, something someone said or something I read.'

When the first couple of articles Emma wrote caused her to receive a deluge of emails she realised that she was right to be writing again. Like many writers, Emma has maintained a portfolio of complementary careers in order to achieve a balance in her life.

'Teaching and journalism fill different needs. I love teaching, I love helping others to learn and inspiring them, but I love writing too. If I dedicate myself to one thing I get bored. I need the mix to keep me interested.'

Her training has taught her to read a story that is already in print and come up with 10 different ideas for updating or adapting it and the publications that might be interested.

'If I'm not feeling particularly creative I pick a random article on any subject and jot down five ideas just to get my mind working. Sometimes I'll take a market and come up with 10 potential article ideas for it. I also go back over my previously published work and look for ways of updating them.'

Though the payment range for journalism can vary widely, Emma would rather write regularly for a smaller publication that pays less but punctually, than have to chase a lucrative market that isn't forthcoming with the pay cheque. The time spent chasing the money makes it just not worth it. Publications usually pay by the 1,000 words and have a set rate, though it is typical for the rate to be between €200 and £200 per thousand words.

Although a natural networker, she did not join any of the networks that were available in Milan.

'I didn't make friends easily in Milan. I just didn't have time. When I was a journalist I was particularly lonely. Ironic given that I was constantly interviewing people,' she says.

Emma finds much of her writing work through her contacts but she also keeps her eyes open at all times for English–language publications all over the world. She specialises in fashion, profiles, how–to and expatriate related work and has been published widely including, The Guardian (www.guardian.co.uk), Living Abroad (www.livingabroadmagazine.com), Eurograduate (www.eurograduate.com), Trip (www.trip–magazine.co.uk) and Transitions Abroad (www.transitionsabroad.com).

Without any initial investment Emma has allowed her ventures to grow organically. Her enthusiasm for her creations has inspired countless others to help her out. It was her initial meetings with Italian women that formed the foundations for the real–time networking, purely because there were few expat women on the island.

Again, Emma continues to add new ideas to her portfolio. Her teaching experience has been useful as she now runs a range of workshops and seminars that she calls 'Business Building in Italy', 'Swapping City Stress for Beach Address' and 'Loving Life in Italy'. She runs them in a hotel in Cannigione and people can book and pay via her website, which uses the secure Paypal (www.paypal.com) system to receive payments. She charges €349 for a two day workshop.

Mario has joined Emma in the Howtoitaly venture and they work with corporate or individual clients helping them to relocate to Italy and have a team of expat relocation consultants all over the island. Their services range from *recce* visits to repatriation. They also consult with individuals who want to relocate to Italy and together they come up with a strategy for the clients. For this they charge from €90 an hour.

A year ago Emma started writing books too. After reading and reviewing lots of publications about living and working in Italy, she decided it was time to write one herself. Mario is a business consultant and manager and writes and speaks about Italian business as part of his job. With Emma's writing skills it made sense that they co–author a book they call *'Running a Business in the Bel Paese'*.

'I don't know how the book will sell,' she says. 'But it will be the first book of its kind. No other book has ever dealt exclusively with setting up a business in Italy. Rather, only a few pages (if that) have been dedicated to the subject.'

Her book review work had led to a friendship with the publicity manager at How To Books and Emma's first job was to see what her contact there thought of her idea. By May she had sent in a proposal and was asked to show a list of chapters to the editorial director. In August they signed the contract. The 80,000 word manuscript has to be with the publisher in March 2006 and will be published the following September.

While publishers typically pay authors a royalty of between seven and 10 per cent of net receipts, most will offer authors favourable discounts if they buy copies for themselves to sell, known as 'buy–back'. Most publishers will offer between 35% and 50% discount, so Emma expects this to be quite a money–spinner for them.

'I did think about self–publishing but knew that with all of my other activities, I wouldn't be disciplined enough to write the book as I would concentrate on all the other strands of the business, including writing articles. Plus in common with friends who are newspaper hacks turned authors, I need a deadline, which isn't self–imposed. The nearer I come to that deadline, the more stress I'm under and the better I write although I'll still agonise over which word is the most appropriate. Having an outside publisher makes me do that,' says Emma.

Discipline and motivation are two traits that freelance writers need by the bucketload and Emma stays on track to meet her publishing deadline thanks to her best friend who is a project manager at IBM. She demands that Emma send her copy on a weekly basis.

'Writing books is new to me but I like it and am working on a second book called *'Loving Life in Italy'*. I suppose it's the same as going on a long holiday to country where you get to really know the place and a quick weekend break where you just see the main features of a city. Writing a book is in depth whereas an article just touches the surface.

'I have all kinds of ideas whirring away in my head and I write them all down in a furry purple book with a monkey face on! And if I see articles that may be of use now or in the future they get torn out and put in my Box of Inspiration. I don't worry about whether or not the ideas are winners or losers as I'm the only one that sees what I've written. Every now and then I go through the box and book and look at what I've collected and written which helps me generate more ideas.

Emma now plans to write a book a year and will soon explore the realms of self–publishing and print on demand rather than working with a publisher.

In Sardinia Emma and Mario have two homes: one in the capital, Cagliari and another in Cannigione 200 metres from the sea. In Cagliari she has a home office but in Cannigione she works at her laptop on the kitchen table, the patio or in a bar.

'If I am writing, I sit on the beach as it inspires me more,' she says. 'I grew up in Poole and Bournemouth and my first memories are of playing on the beach. Living in a tourist destination seems normal to me and living by the sea keeps me motivated. I can only stand to be away for about six weeks.'

Emma's initiative in Sardinia is an inspiration to those who find themselves in a similar position, in a location with no existing networks. And if no network exists, there is every reason to create your own. And in so doing you will make yourself some good friends into the bargain.

EMMA WOULD LIKE TO SHARE THE FOLLOWING

You can contact Emma on: emma.bird@howtoitaly.com

Websites

Weaveweb: www.weaveaweb.it

HowtoItaly: www.howtoitaly.com

GenXpat: www.genxpat.com

Books

Hampshire, D, *Buying a Home in Italy,* Survival Books

Bird, E and Berri, M *Starting a Business in Italy: How to set up and run a successful business in the Bel Paese*, How To Books (publication date September 2006)

Hashemi, S and Hashemi, B *Anyone Can Do It,* Capstone Publishing Ltd

Moore, P *Vroom with a View*, Bantam

Stewart, C *Driving Over Lemons*, Sort of Books

Williams, N *The Work We Were Born to Do*, Element Books

Truss, L *Eats, Shoots & Leaves: The Zero Tolerance Approach to Punctuation*, Profile Books Ltd

Magazines taking articles of expatriate interest

Living Abroad: www.livingabroadmagazine.com

Trip: www.trip–magazine.co.uk

Eurograduate: www.eurograduate.com

Transitions Abroad: www.transitions–abroad.com

The Guardian: www.guardian.co.uk

Living Abroad Report: www.livingabroadreport.com

Xpat Journal: www.xpat.nl

Away: www.awaymagazine.be

The Weekly Telegraph: www.expat.telegraph.co.uk

Expatica: www.expatica.com and www.expatica.com/hr

Organisations

International Teaching and Training Centre: www.ittc.co.uk or tefl@ittc.co.uk

Professional Women's Association: www.pwa–milan.org

Federation of American Women's Clubs Overseas: www.fawco.org

TalentedWomen: www.talentedwomen.com

Ecademy: www.ecademy.com

Linked In: www.linkedin.com

Emma's Tips

Say 'yes' to every opportunity.

Recognise your motives for being a writer – is it to earn money, gain publicity or for the satisfaction of being in print?

If you want a career in writing do not write for free.

Build up your cuttings.

A writer may only be as good as his or her network of contacts.

SIV HARESTAD

Key Information

Body Reflexologist and Teacher

Age: 36

Nationality: Norwegian

Status: Divorced with one son

Countries lived in: Norway, Germany, Spain

Qualifications: Diploma in body reflexology from the Kairon School of Body Reflexology

Years on the move: 5

There is no better marketing tool than a success story, especially when you are personally involved in it.

Fifteen years ago Siv Harestad was suffering from acute tendonitis in her right arm, back pain and constant headaches, caused by working in a stressful sign–making business where, as Siv explains, 'clients always wanted their results to have been delivered yesterday.' Like many people Siv initially took the route of conventional medicine, first trying painkillers, then a chiropractor, and finally a physiotherapist. However, despite investing a serious amount of time and money in the search for a cure Siv continued to suffer. It wasn't until some 18 months after her problems first started that Siv's mother finally managed to persuade her to try some complementary therapy. With a vast array of therapies available, she decided to try body reflexology.

After eight treatments, taken twice a week over just one month, Siv was cured. Most people think of reflexology as a treatment that concentrates on the feet – and indeed, body reflexology does use this method. But rather than isolating a single area it focuses on the many extra reflex points that are to be found all over the body, particularly the chest, arms, legs and ears.

Body reflexology is in Siv's words 'body psychology', originating in Egypt it is the belief that the body communicates through the external manifestation of pain. Different types of pain, occurring in different areas reflect the various problems our body is experiencing.

Siv was so impressed by the therapy that had cured her that she decided she had to find out more. And so Siv decided to train to become a body reflexologist herself. She enrolled at the Kairon school, which although based in Sweden had practitioners in Stavanger, Norway where Siv was living. As if to prove that this was the right choice Siv learnt that the therapist who had cured Siv's ailments would be the one who trained her. This pattern of cause and effect is one that continues to repeat itself in Siv's life and work.

'Before I began to work in this field, I had believed that a body was just a body,' remembers Siv. 'I could not see the connections between psychological and physical disturbances. Now, I am convinced that the mind has a direct influence on the body and it has become my life's work to help people to understand this and be in control of their lives and their well–being.'

Over the years and through the positive feedback she receives from her clients, Siv has developed the skill and wisdom that has allowed her to help countless clients. Many have been heard to comment that she performs miracles.

Her work in Stavanger, Norway, a popular expatriate community, led Siv to take on several foreign clients. This exposure to other cultures gave her the incentive to become an expatriate herself.

'I had been married, divorced, had a child, an apartment, a nice car and so on – but I was feeling stuck. I decided I needed to take my work to another level and went to Germany.'

A firm believer in doing what feels right and following her intuition, Siv decided to leave her 14 year old son behind in Norway with her ex–husband and move to Heidelberg where she would further her studies and practise body reflexology. Siv had previously moved to Germany in order to study medicine, but problems with her papers led to this plan being indefinitely shelved whilst life took over. As Siv says;

'It might seem strange to some people that a mother would leave her son but I had to make a change in my life; I was not satisfied, I thought it would be better for my son to have a happy mother further away than an unhappy mother close by.'

Importantly, Siv's son has always known that he could join his mother at any time should he want to.

Before she left for Germany, Karl–Axel Lind, the founder of Kairon, entrusted Siv with the task of taking body reflexology to the rest of the world. Since then, wherever Siv goes to give treatments, she also finds students.

Putting trust in her instinct yet again, in June 2001, Siv chose to visit one of her British clients, who had since repatriated to England. She wanted to find some students in Gatwick, England, whom she could teach about Kairon. Arriving with no appointments at all, Siv left England two weeks later with three students and a number of satisfied new clients.

With clients now in Germany, Spain, Norway and England, Siv splits her time between each country. Fate has now also led her to Lincolnshire in England, where she now has students too and more than 20 eager clients. 'It's not difficult finding clients as people recognise their own destructive habits and will try anything to be more happy and flexible in their own lives.'

Just a year after she first set foot in England, Siv's first three students qualified and were ready to practise officially.

'I know I am shy by nature, and no one would have believed that I would dare to speak in public about Kairon, but I just take every opportunity that comes my way. I have now spoken about Kairon in English too. If an opportunity pops up and I have time to do it, then I say yes automatically, without thinking.'

Her attitude has now led her to go to Israel as a visiting lecturer, so it will only be a matter of time before there are Kairon students there too.

Not only can this therapy be used to help individuals, Siv has also achieved success in the corporate world. Giving short, half hour, balancing treatments to employees, just twice a week for a month, she has watched morale and motivation rise – and with them profits.

'When I first performed this in a small company, in Norway, I used to telephone them once a month after the treatment, and just watched everything get better and better.'

Siv loves her portable career and is delighted to be able to share her skills with others, giving them in turn a portable career of their own. As she points out, 'You don't need much equipment and can perform it anywhere. It's as flexible as you are.' Body reflexology uses a series of little plastic sticks, which weigh next to nothing, to access the reflex points in the body. When she travels, she takes no special massage bed with her. Instead, she is happy to place a duvet on a kitchen table and work there. In 2004 she moved to Barcelona.

In 2006 she is publishing her first book, *'Cutting the Cords'*, which is published by Bookshaker (www.bookshaker.com).

'It feels fantastic to be free,' she says, having created what she calls her 'fairytale life', free from any ties and constraints.

SIV WOULD LIKE TO SHARE THE FOLLOWING

You can contact Siv on: Sivharestad@hotmail.com

Visit Siv's website at: www.highlevelteam.com

Books

Redfield, J *The Celestine Prophecy*, Bantam

Redfield, J *The Tenth Insight*, Bantam

Revill, M *A Vision of Pearls*, iUniverse.com

St Germain et al, *Saint Germain on Alchemy,* Summit University Press

Jeffers, S *Feel the Fear and Do it Anyway*, Rider & Co

Websites

You can find out about Karl–Axel Lind and Kairon, if you can read Swedish at: www.alternativmedicin.se or www.naturmedicinska.com

Siv's Tips

Watch your food: Don't eat food that makes you tired.

Choose your friends: Use your time on people that make you happy.

Breathe fully: Breathe with your tummy, not your chest.

Be friendly: Smile at a stranger every day.

SUE VALENTINE

Key Information

Food Scientist, Consultant, Writer, Marketer and Photographer

Age: 51

Nationality: British

Status: Married with two children

Countries lived in: India, Sultanate of Oman and England

Qualifications: Bachelor of Science Applied Biology, PhD in Food Science

Years on the move: 8

When Sue embarked on a career as a food scientist she never dreamed she would end up as a writer and photographer: 'But that's expatriate life for you,' she says. Sue originally spent six years as a research and development technologist for a food research association followed by eight years with a drinks vending company in a series of management roles. When she went abroad, she moved into freelance work.

Expatriate life has had a tremendous influence on Sue's career, particularly when you take into account that she had her first baby just before leaving for Oman. Before leaving England, she had been in a highly responsible management position. Whereas starting her new life in Oman, she felt she was 'a nobody.' Nevertheless, opportunities eventually came her way and Sue became a consultant, a writer and a marketer.

Nearly all the contracts Sue has won have contained an element of food science, but her written and verbal communication skills, her determination and her common sense have undoubtedly helped too. To find work, Sue did plenty of networking, mainly at social events and cocktail parties. She told as many people as she could what she did.

'I used to approach decision makers, often over a dinner table having met them a few times, and make suggestions that could lead to a job for me,' explains Sue. 'I began projects that had an unknown result. I took risks. I was also prepared to be flexible.'

Finding regular work in Oman is illegal if you don't have a local sponsor. You can't advertise or knowingly make money without one. But Sue didn't let this get in her way. When she was offered the chance to do some food hygiene training for a local company she approached the British Council. Training is one of their objectives, so she asked them for sponsorship as a consultant and was lucky. They struck an agreement where Sue would make herself available to any of their clients and they would organise her work visa. As is standard in Oman, Sue was obliged to pay them a percentage of her earnings, but she thought this worthwhile.

A career in food science can be portable: food is found everywhere and the food industry is a developing one (as with most industries though, men are still better paid than women). Sue has managed to find plenty of work, and knew she could always have worked as a laboratory technician. Her food hygiene knowledge has proved extremely useful, as training in this subject is essential all over the world.

Sue has a Bachelor of Science degree, which she found fundamental in convincing prospective clients to offer her work. Her experience as a trainer was another plus point. Her PhD helped her to be taken seriously, particularly in a male oriented country such as Oman.

'Doing a PhD gives you a wider view and the invaluable experience of instigating, carrying out to completion, and writing up and editing a project. You can then apply that to anything,' she says.

Sue became interested in writing when she decided with a friend, Jo Parfitt, to publish a book called '*Dates*'. A chance conversation saw a friend complaining that in a country so full of dates she still had no idea what to do with them. This was all it took to spur Sue and Jo on to writing their successful publication.

'I had already followed a short course on creative writing, and felt I was capable of such a large undertaking,' she comments. Sue was responsible for food styling and worked with the photographers, fuelling an interest in photography which had already been awakened by the amazing scenery in Oman. She began to take photography seriously and built up a collection of slides. With her confidence boosted by the date book, she decided to try selling articles and the accompanying photographs.

Like many expatriate accompanying partners before her, in Oman, Sue felt she was a 'big fish in a small pond' and enjoyed all the opportunities that afforded her.

'It is relatively easy to get a lucky break when there are few other writers and photographers around. I cut my teeth on local magazines and although it was marvellous for my ego, I feel that they are not quite on a par with international publications,' she explains.

Sue and Jo published '*Dates'* themselves – in fact they consider it their greatest achievement in Oman. Self–publishing meant they received all the profit, but they had to organise all the marketing and publicity too. Sue offered tastings in supermarkets, gave talks, contacted all the newspapers to achieve as much free editorial as possible and even sold the book at local craft fairs. It wasn't all plain sailing though. To publish '*Dates*', Sue and Jo had to be an official publishing company. They found a local service company to do all their paperwork, handle their accounts and ensure that the book was approved by the Ministry of Information. The company also helped them with the Arabic translation. As Sue was not being paid while working on the book, the British Council, her sponsors, could not object to her diversifying role.

Then the team found a sponsor to underwrite the printing costs. Their guardian angel came in the form of a company called Tamoor Oman, who manufacture date syrup and fibre. This was a new company and they wanted to launch their factory to coincide with the Sultan of Oman's Silver Jubilee. As '*Dates*' was due out at the same time the company could use the book as a promotional tool and gain extra publicity.

'When we published '*Dates*', we became celebrities for a few weeks. We were interviewed for the radio and we saw (28) the front page of the local paper. It's really not that hard to achieve this much in a place like Oman,' she says.

After '*Dates*' was published, Tamoor Oman, asked Sue to join them to be responsible for product development, marketing and demonstrating their products. She also set up and attended exhibitions for them in India and Dubai. She thrived on being able to work with people and found organising and presenting exhibitions exciting. Her career has been enriched by her experiences abroad, but she has hated leaving family and friends back home and sometimes struggled without their support, finding it instead in new companions and colleagues. She reads plenty of self–help and self–discovery books, and knows her time abroad has equipped her with self–reliance and confidence.

In 1997 the Valentines returned to England for a few years. Repatriation helped Sue to feel more aware of what she really wanted to do. This included working from home, writing and photojournalism. Before long she was writing cookery columns for a local magazine and for Women's Business magazine. She also worked on product development for a date importer and did training and consultancy in food safety systems for several companies.

But in 2001, Sue's husband was seconded to India for two years, she had to give up her consultancy and think again! She decided that a period of settling in was again required – Bombay (Mumbai) took some getting used to – but after a year she joined the British Business Group and gradually started networking.

'This time abroad, I decided to settle us all first, get to know some friends by joining clubs and activities, and then think about work,' she says.

As soon as she started to network it became apparent there was lots of work in training, food quality management and technology consultancy – particularly for firms wishing to export to the UK and Europe and restaurants interested in the expatriate and tourist market. Sue started by helping a restaurant to upgrade their quality system and train their staff in formal food safety qualifications. Another project led her to be involved in a project in Abu Dhabi concerned with product development and, ironically, the marketing of date syrup. Over time Sue and her associates found themselves forming an Indian branch of a consultancy with Sue in a technical role. Interest in their services was high.

However, before she knew it, it was time to move back to UK again. This time, because she had kept up her work contacts, after the children had returned to school, she went to work with an old friend and colleague – another consultant who had work to which she could adapt her skills. Sue was very lucky that the work could be done in her home office and in the time she had available when the children were at school. This work eventually led to some business trips in Europe to undertake food safety audits, in which she now specialises.

While Sue has always taken courses to bring up her skills in the area she was working but mostly she learnt as she worked. Most recently, she qualified to be a 3rd party auditor for food safety systems and will be working for one of the most respected audit bodies.

Sue's advice to any budding food scientist destined for a life on the move is simple; be adaptable to your environment; be able to work with as little equipment as possible; use your initiative; and always look at the whole picture.

SUE WOULD LIKE TO SHARE THE FOLLOWING

You can contact Sue on: sue.valentine1@btopenworld.com

Organisations

The Institute of Food Science and Technology (UK)
5 Cambridge Court
210 Shepherd's Bush Road
London
W6 7NJ
Tel: +44 (0)207 6036316
www.ifst.org

Food and Beverage Industry Training Organisation
Training and Careers Executive
6 Catherine Street
London
WC2 5JS

Tel: +44 (0)207 836 2460
www.foodandbeveragetraining.com

British Institute of Professional Photography
Fox Talbot House
2 Amwell Road
Ware
Herts
SG12 9HN
Tel +44 (0)1920 464011
www.bipp.com

National Council for the Training of Journalists
Latton Bush Centre
Southern Way
Harlow
Essex
CM18 7BL
Tel: +44 (0)1279 430009
www.nctj.com

Books

Johnson, S *Who Moved my Cheese*, Vermilion

Harry Paul et al. *Fish*, Coronet Books

Lindenfield, G *Self Esteem*, HarperCollins

Lindenfield, G *Assert Yourself*, HarperCollins

Sue's Tips

Be positive: Remember that moving gives you the chance for a new start – take every opportunity and keep open, enthusiastic and flexible to adapt your skills and learn new skills relevant to the new environment.

Be balanced: You need to have a work/life balance when you move. Once your family are settled, you will feel more settled and you will be more ready to seize work opportunities.

Take it slowly: Don't try to rush making new friends. Keep in contact with your long–standing friends and talk to them. Follow your interests and settle the family and friendship will follow.

Get stationery: Have some cards printed as soon as you have contact numbers.

FINN SKOVGAARD

Key Information

Relocation Expert, Writer and more

Age: 44

Nationality: Danish

Status: Married

Countries lived in: Denmark, England, Luxembourg, Germany and France

Qualifications: Danish Studendereksamen (equivalent of GCSE A levels, diploma in French language

Years on the move: 11

A desire to experience new cultures and to escape what had become a general boredom of his native Denmark led Finn Skovgaard to uproot at the age of 33. Since his initial move in December 1993, this one–time computer specialist has now lived in five different countries and has built up a broad spectrum of micro–careers, each of which can be packed up in his suitcase, ready to go, each time he moves on.

Finn now has so many careers on the boil that in many cases, he cannot even remember what got many of them started.

'Back in 1996 or 1997, I started toying with the idea of writing a book about how to move about in Europe, based on my own experience as a contractor in the IT sphere,' he explains. 'Then, shortly before moving to Paris in 1998 to commence a contract, I discovered the Weekly Telegraph for expats. They invited me to become a mentor when they noticed that I often answered questions about France in their forum,' he recalls.

'Then when I arrived in Paris, I noticed that the estate agent paid an English person to help me search for a flat. I realised I could do that too and when my IT contract ended in Oct 2000, I further developed the idea of providing expat assistance services, getting help with the practical aspects of becoming independent from the French job centre. In 2002, a potential client passed me the price list of a competing, larger company in Paris providing similar services. I later discovered that the business idea, which is known as relocation, was apparently initiated in the USA in the 1990s.'

Aside from his role as a relocation expert, Finn can also add translator and freelance writer to his list of guises, translating user–manuals for consumer or industrial products between Danish, French and English.

'I'm still quite a fledgling when it comes to the writing but I have sold an article to the *Weekly Telegraph* and two to *www.Transitionsabroad.com*, writing about expat subjects.'

Not one to be pigeon–holed however, Finn also runs his own minibus transport service.

'I see this as a secondary activity,' explains Finn, 'partially meant to pay for some of the vehicle. I got the idea when I discovered that only a part of the car cost was tax deductible unless the car was necessary for delivering a service, such as transport.' He then researched the requirements for obtaining a licence for passenger transport and got one. He has consequently transported VIPs in Lille and in Provence, with requests coming mainly from tourists.

'This is a non–intellectual activity that relaxes the brain and gets me out of the house,' he adds.

Perhaps part of the secret to Finn's success with his moveable career is his ability to be flexible and to sniff out and seize any opportunities that come his way.

'I deliberately provide a host of different services in order to be independent of market fluctuations in any one activity,' he explains 'and also to vary my activity. However, they are all more or less related to foreigners or foreign languages.'

Finn certainly maintains the variety, for besides his three main niches, he also boasts a number of mini sidelines. When an expat client asked for a European Accident Statement form in English, since he couldn't understand the French one his French car insurer had given him, Finn found out which printers produced them and bought 100 forms that he now sells online. He also acts as an agent for a low–cost phone call provider in France earning himself commissions on all invoicing for the life of the contract as well as earning commission on medical insurance he manages to sell to expats in France, for the duration of the contracts.

You may think that spinning so many plates at one time may prove quite an arduous task. Not so. Finn runs all of his businesses from a room in his house.

'This way there's no loss in commuting time and cost,' he explains. 'It also means I don't have to think about rent and it's easier to adapt flexible working hours.'

The list of equipment necessary to keep all of the businesses going is minimal too. Finn survives on a computer, printer, scanner, photocopier, minibus and dictionaries and estimates that it cost him under £1,000 to get started.

He does rely heavily on the Internet and marketing though, and puts quite a heavy emphasis on these. Finn has his own Internet site and focuses on search engine optimisation, that's to say, making sure he receives a good ranking on Google and other search engines. He also maintains a presence on expat sites and portals through forum activity or free or paid articles and finally, letting word–of–mouth work by making all efforts never to leave a client dissatisfied.

'Unfortunately, the professional education fund that I have to pay to in France prioritises technical education, not marketing,' he muses 'and this is something I really can't understand. What good is it to have the world's best services if you don't know how to sell them?'

Finn does love the freedom a portfolio of portable careers has afforded him though. 'I would hate to have to go back into an office,' he says, 'for example to direct a small number of employees if turnover allowed that. I would hate to go back to employment or employment–like contracting where I'd be told what to do. That said, if someone else were considering a portable career, I would recommend acquiring skills that are generally useful in more than one single country or that can be used for providing services at distance, for example, translation, marketing, business in general, computing or medicine. If possible, avoid being entirely dependent on one single skill or business sector. Don't put all your eggs in one basket. In today's dynamic and global market, it's as true as ever.'

FINN WOULD LIKE TO SHARE THE FOLLOWING

You can contact Finn on: finn@skovgaard–europe.com

Websites

www.skovgaard–europe.com/linkexpatfrance.htm has a long list of expat resource sites

Translation sites

Translators Café: www.translatorscafe.com

Go Translators: www.gotranslators.com

Proz: www.proz.com

Translation Zone: www.translationzone.com

Finn's Tips

If searching for a change of career, how do you determine what to do? There is no single good answer, but what I did was to ask myself the following questions:

If I stop my current career, which other skills do I then have that I can use for working? Think back to school and think about where you got medium–to–good marks. For example, I was good at maths and so originally chose IT as my profession. But I also liked writing certain type of texts and I liked languages. These skills led to freelance writing and translation on topics about expat life. Ability to organise led me to open and run a small business and to organise my expat life. When considering this, be creative and do a brain storming session. Do it when relaxed.

What do I want to do? Which of these skills would I like to work with and find inspiring?

How might I earn a living from my skills? Which of the remaining skills could provide a living?

NANCY MAYER

Key Information

A musical career; singing and teaching

Age: 39

Nationality: American

Status: Married

Countries lived in: America and The Netherlands

Qualifications: Bachelor of Music in voice performance from Oberlin Conservatory of Music and a Master of Music in voice performance from the Eastman School of Music

Years on the move: 10

All Nancy Mayer had ever wanted to do was sing. Having taken voice lessons from the age of 15 and having gone on to receive both Bachelor's and Master's degrees in voice performance from colleges in the United States, Nancy has made sure that music has always been a part of her life. And it was music that brought her to The Netherlands in 1995 too. Albeit indirectly.

'My boyfriend, Jonathan, (now husband) came to study at the conservatory in The Hague – he was a musician too, studying violin –, and I decided that a change of country might be a great idea for my music career as well,' she says.

A decade later and Nancy is still enjoying life in the lowlands as a classical singer, specialising in early music: medieval, renaissance and baroque, and as a singing teacher. Nancy sings concerts with different ensembles in concert series both in the Netherlands and throughout Europe and teaches amateur students how to use their voices and bodies better for singing. In fact, being in The Netherlands has allowed Nancy to concentrate on doing exactly what she loves. In America, she had to hold down three jobs to support her one passion.

'I was a classical singer, as well as a secretary and the superintendent of an apartment building,' she explains. 'If I were still in America now, I'd definitely have to have some kind of office job to supplement my income, as I just couldn't make a living from being a singer or a teacher. Having that job would then make it harder to have energy for practising and preparing for concerts and would give me less time for students.'

Here in The Netherlands, Nancy is able to earn around €350 per concert as a solo singer. This may sound like a lot, but as Nancy explains, 'this can mean anything from a day to a week of rehearsals, which is included in that price, so, hourly, it doesn't work out to much, especially as I have to prepare the music before I even start rehearsing. It's difficult to support oneself on such a low fee'. Nevertheless, Nancy has now sung professionally for 16 years with choirs, and as a soloist with chamber music groups and in opera productions and feels that she learns to sing better with every concert. She finds however, that it's her work as a singing teacher that is more lucrative.

'I charge €30 per 45 minute lesson, which is a good hourly wage although my students tend to come every two weeks, so I have to have a lot of students to make a regular weekly income.'

Thankfully though, teaching is somewhere Nancy feels as at home as she is a singer herself and she has being teaching for seven years now. Again, this is something Nancy feels she has improved upon year on year.

'Throughout my life, I've had some fantastic teachers who have informed and inspired me to do the same', she says. 'I am an accomplished singer and I love to perform – I am a good communicator and enjoy expressing something to an audience, but I also love the teaching. I am fascinated by the psychology of what makes different people open up and be able to sing and express themselves – I am insightful and a good listener, not only to what a student's voice sounds like, but what might be keeping them from singing their best.' In fact for Nancy, watching a student open up the part of themselves that enables them to use their voice and sing has proved to be one of her most gratifying achievements.

Although keeping the work on an even flow has proved tricky at times for Nancy, she markets her singing mainly through word of mouth and reputation.

'Colleagues I have already worked with recommend me to other groups who are looking for a singer,' she explains, 'or sometimes I do auditions. I get students for lessons mainly through word of mouth too,' she says. Although Nancy also belongs a networking group based in The Hague, she still finds that her work goes in waves. 'To find more regular students, I'll have to advertise in many more places,' she concedes.

Being freelance does have its benefits though. For one thing it has meant that she has time to spend with her children, three–year–old Claire Ellen and one–year–old Sammy. It also means that her lifestyle is incredibly varied.

'I really have no such thing as a typical day,' she says. 'My morning may consist of some practice and translating texts, and in the afternoon I would be teaching students. Of course, I may have a lot or no students at all, depending on whether I have a concert to prepare for.' However, the nature of her work does mean that if concerts or students cancel, she makes no money at all. For anyone else considering a portable career in singing, Nancy advises that networking is probably the best way to get work for both performing and teaching.

'For singing it's really best to be doing concerts; then the more people who know me, and hear me sing, the better chance I'll have of finding work or that the work will come to me,' she says.

Aside from networking, Nancy recommends learning languages so she can understand, and therefore feel, what she is singing and taking Alexander Technique lessons which help use the body for singing in an optimal way. Although she has lost track of what it cost her to get her business running, the start–up costs were relatively lo. She conducts the singing lessons from home, which reduces her overheads significantly and her professional equipment consists of an electric piano, a computer, dictionaries in various languages, music scores and concert clothing when needed.

'Audition for anyone who will hear you and do lots of concerts to meet other musicians,' she advises. 'And go out and meet people and make contacts as soon as possible – you never know who will connect you with someone who can help your business.'

Like many expats, Nancy has discovered that teaching something you do and love yourself can be the perfect portable career.

NANCY WOULD LIKE TO SHARE THE FOLLOWING

You can contact Nancy on: nmayer@ensbraccio.com

Books

Kagen, S *On Studying Singing*, Dover Publications

Ristad, E *A Soprano on Her Head*, Real People Press

Timothy McGee, et al, *Singing Early Music*, Indiana University Press (a guide on pronunciation of European languages in the late Middle Ages and Renaissance)

Websites

Connecting Women: a network for professional and internationally aware women, based in The Hague, The Netherlands.

www.connectingwomen.nl

Nancy's Tips

Network as much as possible.

Don't be afraid to promote yourself.

Feel entitled to work in a foreign country.

BILLY ALLWOOD

Key Information

Running an Expat Website

Age: 45

Nationality: British

Status: Divorced with three children

Countries lived in: England, Brazil and The Netherlands

Qualifications: BSc and PhD in Chemistry

Years on the move: 12

With a PhD in chemistry, it would be feasible to envisage Billy Allwood shut away in a laboratory somewhere, wearing a white coat, ferreting away on the latest scientific breakthrough. In fact, this image couldn't really be further from Billy's reality. Far from living in isolation, he has made a career out of socialising. As the brainchild behind the fledgling website, The Hague Online, it is Billy's mission to keep fellow expats of The Hague constantly informed of anything that is worth knowing or doing in the City.

It was his work in the computer industry, post studying, that first took Billy Allwood overseas to Rio de Janeiro in 1991 for a couple of years. Later, his role with a Brazilian company in the business software industry based in London brought him to The Hague in 1994. It wasn't until much later however, that Billy considered putting his IT knowledge to good use for the benefit of the whole of The Hague's English–speaking community.

As a socialite at heart, and a divorcee whose children no longer live with him, Billy liked to keep abreast of and participate in the social events in his hometown.

'The idea for The Hague Online only really came to me because I was wandering around the Statenkwartier – an area in The Hague with a large expat population – and saw a poster for a Murphy's Comedy night which had already passed,' he explains. And, in true entrepreneurial spirit, Billy set about thinking of a solution.

'I just started thinking about how companies could communicate with expats in The Hague, creating a symbiotic relationship between expats and businesses,' he says. And so the concept of The Hague Online was born.

Still only a year old, The Hague Online is a website for expats, by expats and is constantly updated with daily headlines and news on current and forthcoming events occurring in and around The Hague. But word of the site has spread like wildfire. Billy claims this is through word of mouth, although in truth, it probably has more than a little to do with his incessant and almost subconscious ability to network.

'I network by attending as many social functions as I possibly can,' he says. However, Billy's approach to networking is pretty informal. 'I don't belong to any specialised networking clubs – just the squash club,' he laughs. Although Billy's approach is obviously having an impact as the site is now attracting over 18,000 readers a month.

That's not to say that getting the site to this stage has all been plain sailing. In addition to the €10,000 it cost to set the site up, it also took a heavy investment in time – between six and nine months – before Billy really started to feel that the website was on its way.

'In fact, I am still investing in the site,' he says, 'and it is only through positive support from members of the expat community that I have been able to get so far,' he says.

Unsurprisingly, there are several elements involved in successfully running a venture such as this. 'It is a social job,' says Billy, 'but there's also an awful lot of behind the scenes work too that are fundamental to the survival of the site.'

Writers have to be sourced, articles commissioned, edited and occasionally translated. In addition, there are the sales and administration to be done, not to mention the promotion of the site. And although Billy's cheeky chappie personality and natural networking have attracted readers to the site almost by osmosis, attracting advertisers has proved to require a much more proactive approach.

'I generally only hook in advertisers by contacting them myself,' he says, 'and it's upon these advertisers that the survival of the site is financially reliant as there is no subscription fee to readers.'

Thankfully, Billy's previous experience as managing director for a business software company in The Hague has left him equipped to deal with all of these tasks, which is lucky, as up until now, the venture has seen him carrying out a large proportion of the work himself. For Billy, this is perhaps the worst part of the job. As director, although it is important for him to get out and meet expats and company owners, the other sides of the business mean that for the time being, he is largely chained to his living room from where he is responsible for running and promoting the website.

'I'm not the type of person who enjoys working alone,' says Billy. 'This isn't where my main strengths lie. In the future, I really hope to be able to leave the daily running of the website to a journalist, so that I can concentrate on organising activities and doing what I do best.'

And there seems to be plenty of organisational scope brimming in Billy, just waiting to be let out. Following the success of the site, Billy recently created The Supper Club, a weekly event for expats to meet other expats that takes place in a different restaurant in The Hague each week.

'This is great,' says Billy. 'It gives members the chance to move around The Hague sampling all the culinary delights the city has to offer whilst simultaneously building up a new network of friends.' In fact, this event has proved so popular since its inception that Billy now boasts a growing number of Dutch members too.

Although the project has proved to be a huge task, Billy's boundless energy has got him through and he is thankful of the new–found freedom that his role has afforded him. If it wasn't for The Hague Online, Billy knows that he would still be tied to some international company somewhere. From experience though, for anyone considering doing something similar, Billy would recommend trying to form an alliance with someone to share the load and to make sure that you have enough money to fund the project to begin with – as Billy has seen, it can take a while to start reaping the rewards.

BILLY WOULD LIKE TO SHARE THE FOLLOWING

You can contact Billy on: Billy@TheHagueOnLine.com

Websites

The Hague Online: www.TheHagueOnline.com

Networks

Bureau Binnenstad – an organisation set up by the KvK, Stichting Binnenstad and the local authority to promote a positive image of The Hague city centre: www.binnenstad–denhaag.nl

Billy's Tips

Make sure you have some funding in place to see you through the more austere periods at the start of the project.

Make full use of the Internet to inform yourself fully and contact relevant people or companies.

Form alliances with other people or organisations so you can share the cost or responsibility.

KAREN FRENCH

Key Information

A Career in Image Consultancy

Age: 41

Nationality: British

Status: Married with two children

Countries lived in: England, Bahrain, Dubai, Holland, Jakarta and Singapore

Qualifications: A few O–Levels and the International Baccalaureate. Full Image Diploma from Color Me Beautiful (UK), Make up for Brides and Photography from Top to Toe College of Beauty Therapy (Singapore) and a Fashion Merchandising Diploma from International Correspondence School USA.

Years on the move: 37

Having spent 37 of her 41 years relocating, Karen French was almost born on the move and it was clear that if she wanted to earn a living, Karen needed a career she could take with her, wherever she went.

Image consultancy was not something Karen considered immediately. In fact, she had tried her hand at several things before falling upon the idea. She had assisted with exhibitions at the World Trade Centre in Dubai, done a stint in the Middle East Regional Office of Philip Morris and even worked for the Treasury Department of Arab Banking Corporation in Bahrain.

'Although grateful for the experiences,' she explains, 'these were just jobs, certainly not a career.'

After having her first child in 1990, job changes beyond her family's control due the Gulf War and several house and country moves, Karen found herself suffering with low self–esteem.

'After settling into life in Holland with another move to Singapore on the horizon, I decided that if I was ever gong to work again, I had to take my destiny into my own hands. This was when I decided to apply for an Image Training Course with Color me Beautiful in London,' she explains.

It was clear from the start that with Color me Beautiful, Karen had found her niche.

'First and foremost,' she says, 'I am not afraid to work hard. Secondly, I have always been extremely creative, even from the days of playing 'dress–up' with my Barbie dolls, to my current passion of painting on silk. As a child, I'd spend hours cutting pictures of skirts, dresses, lipsticks and shoes out of magazines to paste into scrap books. If only I'd pursued my 'Passion For Fashion' then it would have saved a lot of years doing unfulfilling jobs. To be honest, I always knew deep down that I wanted to do something with women and clothes but had no idea or direction to follow my dreams. A career in the world of Image and Fashion would have seemed absurd in the highly academic school where I studied in the Middle East.

As an image consultant, Karen offers one–to–one and small group workshops on the most flattering colours and styles to wear, she also goes to client's homes and offers advice on wardrobe management. In fact, Karen's business has grown rapidly since the early days and has gone on to incorporate, amongst other things, personal shopping, fashion shows, bridal makeup, makeup and skincare workshops and training.

'I started my business doing colour and style classes. I then did a Fashion Merchandising course and then added Wardrobe Management and Personal Shopping to my services. Later, when I felt more confident, I ventured into clothes co–ordination and assisted in the production of fashion shows. Finally, I teamed up with the importers of an exclusive European skin care product because I liked it and wanted to use it in my business. I then became their freelance trainer and conducted all their in–house training to the salons that bought the product.'

As Karen's business expanded, she decided to rent some space but found that she was spending so little time in the office owing to the services she offered, that even though it gave a more professional image and was prestigious, it wasn't really economical or necessary.

'Even with the office, I found myself taking much of my work home to do once the children had gone to bed,' she says. 'I now work from home and find this fits my needs.'

Karen's business has grown well, although the whole process has been a learning curve. 'There is a danger in this line,' she says, 'to get into too many things, and unless you want to expand and take on more people, as a sole–trader, you have to learn to say 'no'.'

In the early days, Karen found herself saying 'yes' to sponsoring events and would give endless hours to charity fashion shows, even though she had to burn the midnight oil for no financial gain.

'To me, this was free advertising and good exposure,' she explains. 'But as you become more popular and in demand, you need to choose carefully and be more selfish – something I find very hard to do. I now have to ask myself: 'what's in it for me?' or, 'how will it benefit the business?' It has to be a win–win situation so I don't end up burning myself out.'

Thankfully, all the early days of hard work now seem to have paid off and Karen is able to reap the rewards. Karen is also grateful for those earlier experiences in the corporate world too. Attending courses in sales and marketing as well as 'Putting People First', which was run by Time Manager International UK (1987) have stood her in good stead.

'My time in Jakarta as editor for the Australian and NZ Association (ANZA) magazine helped too, especially when it comes to understanding magazine deadlines for my own ads, submitting ad material and using this form of media to enhance my exposure.'

But it is perhaps the networking that has proved instrumental in getting Karen's business to where it is today. 'Fortunately, living an expatriate lifestyle, there are an abundance of events, launches, clubs, women's groups and so on, to assist in making networking a less daunting task.'

Karen warns however, that it is good to focus and choose the events you attend carefully, otherwise you could find yourself spending a lot of money or energy on attending events which could have few prospects.

Although Karen's business is now doing so well, she still runs on relatively little equipment, including a full–length mirror, coloured–fabric drapes, a comfortable chair, stocks of swatches, cosmetics, skin–care supplies and samples.

'In the beginning, I invested in slides and a projector for my talks and presentations. These days I use my Apple Mac Power G4 notebook for my Power Point Presentations – the most fabulous tool for creative people!'

For other people considering a career in image consultancy, Karen would also suggest that a 'good eye' is essential, together with a love of the fashion world, skincare and cosmetics, colours and fabrics and an ability to go against the grain, which means the ability to advise a client on what suits her regardless of your own likes and dislikes.

'I would also suggest that you never stop learning,' she adds. 'I continue to upgrade my skills when I have time and when something related to what I do will enhance the business or services offered.'

Once you are up and running, as Karen's example shows, the world is your oyster. And the money can be good too. Her earnings can range from as little as the profit from a lipstick sale or as much as $2000 per day for a corporate training job.

'But,' says Karen, 'the satisfaction of a happy and grateful client far outweighs the fees earned – just knowing you have made a difference to someone's life or perception of themselves.'

KAREN WOULD LIKE TO SHARE THE FOLLOWING

You can contact Karen on: KarenFrenchDesigns@hotmail.com

Websites

Style Careers: www.stylecareer.com

The Federation of Image Consultants UK: www.tfic.org.uk

Advice on careers and training in Image: www.colourflair.com

Karen's Tips

Self-Motivation is a must.

Surround yourself with positive people.

Never stop learning.

CAROLINE LIEBENOW

Key Information

A career in fine arts and design

Age: 30

Nationality: American

Status: Married to a Finn

Countries lived in: America and Finland

Qualifications: BFA, Bachelor of Fine Arts and a training certificate in entrepreneurship.

Years on the move: 5

Caroline Liebenow had always led a creative existence. Initially after graduating in 1998 she worked as a newspaper reporter and was the chairperson of her town's local chapter of the Massachusetts Cultural council.

In 1999 however, Caroline decided that it was time to broaden her horizons. Spurred on by this nagging urge to 'leave the nest' as she puts it and in search of adventure, she packed her bags and headed for Finland in the autumn of that year.

'I don't know what led me to Finland,' she says. 'I just wanted to go somewhere unusual.'

Since moving to Finland, Caroline has largely relinquished herself of her duties as a local hack and has started up a fine arts and design studio, in which she creates silk and velvet fashion accessories, watercolour paintings, decorative photography and stationery. Although professionally, Caroline has changed direction, her term as the chairperson of the Cultural Council gave her a firm grounding for her new venture.

'It taught me the importance of being well organised, as well as providing me with the basic, but fundamental skills of communication, diplomacy and leadership,' she says.

'It's hard to put into words,' says Caroline, 'why I chose to develop a business in this sector. I guess it stems from childhood. It is like a calling, part of my identity. Whenever I take a break from designing, I feel like something is missing from my life. I am very imaginative and I love creative problem–solving,' she adds. 'I also enjoy analysing what works and what doesn't and why.'

But although the necessary creativity for this venture may have been innate, the practicalities of getting the business off the ground have proved a little more arduous.

'The business idea was part of my plans even before I moved to Finland,' explains Caroline, 'but it took over three years to decide to make the commitment and learn how to set up, where to find the right information, what is required and what isn't and so on.'

The basic start–up costs and investments for such an enterprise are relatively low. Although Caroline started with existing capital and materials, she estimates that it cost her about $1,000 to get up and running and she survives on a computer, scanner, digital camera and printer. Of those, the computer is her fundamental piece of equipment.

'I use it to store most of my financial records, to reproduce images, catalogue designs, and of course to network.' Her only other business tool has been to achieve fluency in the Finnish language, and grow to understand the Finnish business culture.

Having done her research and registered her business, it then took Caroline about a year to start seeing the identity of the business emerge. 'The first six months were difficult because personal reasons took my concentration away from the business, so promotion of the enterprise was delayed.'

And as Caroline has come to learn, face–to–face networking and promotion is one of the most vital factors if you want to ensure success in the world of creative arts.

'I market my business in a number of ways,' says Caroline, 'I have my own website, hand out business cards, use online directories, word–of–mouth and attend trade shows.' Of those, the most effective methods are attending trade shows and word–of–mouth because that is the only way potential customers can see Caroline's work up close and get a real feel for what it's about, whilst existing customers get a chance to see what's new. For a while, Caroline did have a shopping cart feature on her website but stopped using it as soon as she realised that customers in the fine art and design sector really do need to be able to see the creation for themselves. In addition, Caroline feels that it's important for the customer to be able to build up a rapport with the seller who can describe the inspiration behind the work, explain its uniqueness and help the customer decide exactly just what to buy; something that just cannot be achieved electronically.

Networking has made all the difference to Caroline's business and although she still works from a small, basically–equipped corner in her home, Caroline makes a real effort to get out and market herself as often as she can. She attends business–related seminars, gallery–openings and offers advice.

'A Finnish consulting company has recruited me twice within six months as a mentor for two local Finnish women interested in entrepreneurship. The important thing is to always maintain a presence, even if nothing long–term comes out of a particular event,' says Caroline.

For Caroline, part of her success has stemmed from her initial move overseas.

'Ironically,' she says, 'it wasn't until I moved abroad that I learned about the importance of networking – the challenges of living abroad made the necessity apparent. So, even though I'd like to think I would have been making the same progress had I not moved overseas, the reality is that it probably would have taken me longer to learn the same lessons about entrepreneurship, because in my own culture I would have taken such things for granted and not been able to perceive as much growth.'

Although Caroline still considers her business to be at the start–up level, signs of growth are clear from her increased publicity, a more defined image and a more obvious, steady pattern of sales and opportunities. These opportunities have included being interviewed by newspapers, having her work represented in two international shows, her first solo show in Finland and initiating cooperative work with two other art and design entrepreneurs.

As her success continues, Caroline would eventually like to open a shop and add professional writing to her business description.

For anyone else considering a portable career, Caroline would recommend being flexible and open to connections that may bring you opportunities that might not be quite what you had in mind.

'Often it is worth while accepting offers for jobs that weren't really part of your plan, just for the extra income or for the publicity and exposure that can later help to promote your business.'

Whilst building her own business up to the level she would like, Caroline also does some journalism and English teaching on the side, not to mention currently working on the manuscript for a book about her adventures in Finland as well as a Finnish grammar reference book for English speakers. In July 2005 she helped to launch the first English language newspaper in the town of Oulu where she lives. Called 65 Degrees North, it is available online.

As Caroline has learned, it can take years to establish a brand name for yourself and to be earning a decent living. But for her, the wait is well worth it.

'I take real pride in helping to promote the value of handcrafted items. There is the satisfaction of knowing that my name is out there every time I make a sale, in addition to knowing that the customer is making an investment that will someday be a collector's item.'

It was only by moving to live in a rather unusual expatriate location that Caroline was able to work, at last with her passion. Despite living in a community that has a relatively small international community, Caroline has created the perfect portable career. So, she was not at all daunted when she and Heikki moved to the USA in late 2005.

CAROLINE WOULD LIKE TO SHARE THE FOLLOWING

You can contact Caroline on: info@liebenowdesign.com

For more information on Caroline and her portable career visit: www.LiebenowDesign.com

Websites

Arts and crafts: www.artsandcrafts.about.com

65 degrees north: www.65degreesnorth.com

Caroline's Tips

Get into the habit of doing one thing or taking a step – big or small – to promote yourself on a regular basis.

Think about your options to diversify – what else could you do with your existing skills, product or service?

Expect the unexpected. Sometimes the best developments can come from seemingly unlikely resources, and vice versa, that seemingly definite opportunities can lead to disappointment.

KELLY MIDURA

Key Information

A career as a Website Designer

Age: 39

Nationality: American

Status: Married

Countries lived in: America, United Kingdom, Bolivia, Guatemala, Zambia, El Salvador, Czech Republic

Qualifications: BA in Government from Georgetown University

Years on the move: 15, more or less

Although Kelly graduated with a degree in government from Georgetown University, her working life to date bears virtually no relation to her studies. Having married straight out of university, Kelly had never really entered the job market. Whilst she had always found some type of work when abroad, mainly editing embassy newsletters and writing the odd article, she had never developed a career:

'After graduating from university I went into Spanish language training almost immediately and moved to Bolivia with my husband Chris who is a US Foreign Service Officer,' she says.

This all changed when a friend noticed a personal page that she had developed at the Geocities website back in 1998. This led to Kelly being asked to take over the maintenance of the website for the Associates of the American Foreign Service Worldwide (www.AAFSW.com) for a nominal wage. Shortly afterwards another friend asked her to design the original Tales from a Small Planet (www.talesmag.com), which was then called the Sojourner's Underground Network (SUN).

Kelly has picked up all her skills on the job itself and now charges a fee that is commensurate with her experience and has several other clients.

'Although my technical knowledge is less than many website designers and I don't have qualifications specific to this industry, I have always had a good command of the English language, skill, which is notably lacking among technical types. Several clients have been quite grateful that I can write and edit as I design.'

According to Kelly, website design is all about organisation, but it is also very visual. As an amateur artist and a general visual thinker, designing attractive websites comes easily to her.

If she were not abroad, Kelly feels that she would probably work in publishing and would earn just about the same kind of money that she is earning now. She can easily charge $50 an hour, and could charge twice that if she felt she had exceptional technical skills, were willing to handle databases and deal with complicated e–commerce sites.

Perhaps the secret to her success is that Kelly chooses her clients carefully and only works for people who are doing something she finds to be interesting or worthy. These 'worthy' clients only pay Kelly's lower, non–profit rate.

'My personal goal is not so much to make a lot of money, as to make a good hourly wage. I consider my time to be valuable and with children to raise I have deliberately limited the number of clients that I work for,' Kelly is clear that her priority is to have time with her children, Rachel, 14 and Bryant, 10.

The ability to pack her entire office into one box when she moves to her family's next posting, gives her career a distinct advantage and she enjoys the flexibility. On the move since 1989, Kelly has lived in Bolivia, Guatemala, Zambia, El Salvador, Washington DC and the Czech Republic. She recently returned to Washington, DC, where her family will be posted indefinitely.

'The worst thing about my job is that I spend too long staring at a computer and it can be a bit isolating,' she says. 'I don't think I could do this full–time. My art classes, involvement with my children's activities, school functions and so on go some way to making up for a lack of day to day adult contact.'

Kelly's advice to others who want a similarly flexible and portable career, is to 'think outside the box';

'Make sure you choose your clients carefully. Nowadays everyone wants to have a website but few people have enough material to compose one or enough money to finance the design. If you're not careful you can waste a lot of time handing out free advice.'

'If you have decided to follow someone around the world then you have got to be flexible and in my experience those who get too narrowly focused on doing what they are trained to do, or what they did 'before', end up frustrated and miserable.'

According to Kelly, website design is the perfect portable career, as there is rarely a situation in which you need to be physically present. With clients located across the globe, Kelly has even dealt with people who took weeks to realise she was in a different country, let alone a different continent. Although more and more countries have sophisticated Internet connections problems can emerge if you end up in a country with very basic facilities. However, having said that, Kelly has successfully managed to run her business using a 44K dial up.

If you want to take up a career in website design, Kelly suggests that you volunteer to design a site for a local charity, school or non–profit organisation to start with; there is no substitute for hands–on experience. If there is no suitable organisation that needs your help then start by creating your own family website.

For beginners Kelly suggests avoiding Microsoft Front Page, which, although standard on many computers, is very limited. Instead try out a professional web authoring programme like DreamWeaver. For graphics, Paint Shop Pro is perfectly adequate for starting out.

By working initially in a voluntary capacity for an organisation about which she was passionate, Kelly has created a lucrative, flexible and wholly portable career.

KELLY WOULD LIKE TO SHARE THE FOLLOWING

You can contact Kelly on Kelly@midurafamily.org

You can see Kelly's work at the following website: www.midurafamily.org/design.htm

Websites

Associates of the American Foreign Services Worldwide: www.aafsw.com

Tales from a Small Planet: www.talesmag.com

Download a trial version of professional web design software, Dreamweaver, at: www.macromedia.com

Zdnet: www.zdnet.com

Dummies: www.dummies.com

HTML for dummies is invaluable for those starting out

Peachpit: www.peachpit.com

Peachpit press has great books for those who are teaching themselves various aspects of web design

Web developers virtual library: www.wdvl.com

HTML help: www.htmlhelp.com

Getting started in website design

www.hotwired.lycos.com/webmonkey

www.personalweb.about.com/internet/personalweb/cs/tipstools/

Free web space

www.geocities.yahoo.com

www.tripod.lycos.com

Web writing and editing

Contentious: www.contentious.com

Support, advice and inspiration

Webgrrls: www.webgrrls.com

Kelly's Tips

Volunteer. Working for free can be a great way to learn without panicking if you make mistakes.

Ask for help. Never be afraid to ask experts for help. They will usually be flattered.

Use the Internet as a great source of information and free software.

CHRISTINE MILJKOVIC

Key Information

A career as a computer training consultant/teacher

Age: 43

Nationality: British

Status: Married with 3 children

Countries lived in: England, Malaysia, Germany, Russia, Holland, Singapore

Qualifications: 6 CSE's, 2 O–levels and 25 years of computer industry and training experience.

Years on the move: 40

Born to a father who worked in the army, mother of three, Christine Miljkovic, was virtually born moving. Even settling down to married life in 1987 at the age of 23 didn't see an end to Christine's transitory lifestyle. A joint quest for adventure and money saw Christine and her husband, who works in the oil industry, relocating to Russia only a week after marrying.

Christine had already been in the computer industry for 10 years, working with several different companies before starting to travel with her husband. She had already specialised in training in the UK although it wasn't until being begged by friends to train them that she arrived at her current career as a personal computer trainer. Now Christine has a fully–fledged career, which includes visiting the home or office of her customers, assessing whatever kind of training they need and advising them on what they need in terms of software and hardware.

'The training then continues in their home or office,' explains Christine. 'We work on a one–to–one basis, tailoring the training to their exact requirements and working at their own pace. The training can be for one session or 40, depending on what they want to know, how old they are and how fast they learn.' And Christine boasts a whole host of clients, from a sixteen year–old girl to an 88 year–old couple.

For Christine, computer training was the obvious choice for a portable career. Not only does she consider herself to be a very social person, but computer training can be done anywhere in the world and is needed by virtually everyone.

'Coupled with that, I love to help and inspire people, especially women who haven't worked for years and have lost their confidence,' concludes Christine. And, since the Internet explosion and because she is constantly mixing in expat circles, Christine rarely finds herself short of work.

'Expats always need to know how to use email and the Internet, along with some digital photography to understand how to use photographs sent to them,' she explains. She just needs to be sure that she constantly stays ahead of the game when it comes to familiarising herself with new software.

Christine's business retains its portability by being relatively low maintenance; all she needs to keep the business rolling is an up–to–date computer, printer, scanner, digital camera and lots of files, books and stationery. And since she already had a computer when she initially set up the business, her only expenditure when getting started was business cards.

Of course, each new move sees Christine having to start up again. As she does one–to–one tuition, whenever she relocates, her client–base gets left behind. But with each relocation, starting up has got easier and easier.

'It took me about a year and a half to get up and running the first time,' she explains. 'After that, it happened within six months and I had more confidence to market myself after having had my business for 10 years in Singapore.'

Word of mouth alone seems to bring in ample business, without the need to advertise. 'I network by joining a few clubs wherever I am and mentioning what I do,' says Christine. 'I try to go to most things I am invited to, so that I can meet more people – I am by nature a person who likes to be involved in a lot of things and a lot of my networking is done in different social groups.' In fact, Christine finds that networking is invaluable for both her business and for friendships.

'It's actually very hard to network just for business,' says Christine, 'to do it effectively, you have to have a real interest in people. I seem to pick up new customers wherever I go but perhaps this is because I have learnt to be a good listener and how to inspire confidence in people. I have done lots of character analysis courses, but more through interest than through necessity.'

Consequently, Christine has found herself with a continual supply of new friends as a result of her business. 'The friends are the most important to me,' she says, 'as being an expat, people always come and go.' In fact one of the most problematic parts of Christine's job is trying to tell customers that they really don't need any more training. 'Some people just don't want to stop,' she says, 'the classes are social, fun and friendly, especially if you are lonely.'

The business has certainly provided Christine with a lifeline, throughout her numerous international deployments, getting her out of the house, into interesting locations, meeting new people and making new friends. And the income from it all isn't bad either. Christine commands €80 for an hour and a half. And although she admits that if she had never come abroad, she would probably be working in computers for a big company, earning big money, she wouldn't have the flexibility that her current lifestyle affords her.

But for anyone else looking to create a portable career, Christine's best advice would be to choose something you love as just doing it just for the money won't make it fun. Christine almost got sidetracked from her career when a chance meeting with a Sri Lankan lady who happened to like her voice led to Christine recording five CDs to go with five phonics books while she was living in Singapore.

'There are now thousands of children around Asia learning English by listening to my voice,' she explains. 'I was also asked to do some voice–overs afterwards by the recording studio. I had fun, learnt a lot, but chose to stick with computers.'

The rewards have been numerous; one of Christine's greatest achievements was to teach an elderly couple to put 50 years' worth of family tree information from paper onto the computer using old photographs converted to digital output and a file full of papers. As technology is always changing, there will always be something new for Christine to learn and pass on.

CHRISTINE WOULD LIKE TO SHARE THE FOLLOWING

You can contact Christine on: 121pct@planet.nl

Websites

Petroleum Wives Club of The Hague: www.pwc–thehague.com

Connecting Women: www.connectingwomen.nl

Christine's Tips

Be open to new ideas – you may find you can do something you have never thought of.

Never turn down a networking opportunity – something always comes of it, even if it's six months later.

Be positive and enthusiastic about what you do.

BERNADETTE HUYSING

Key Information

A Career as an Internet Retailer

Age: 36

Nationality: Australian

Status: Married

Countries lived in: Australia, The Netherlands

Qualifications: Bachelor of Applied Science, Graduate Diploma in Education BA

Years on the move: 8

Before accompanying her husband overseas in 1997, Bernadette Huysing was enjoying life in Australia as a teacher. Now, nearly a decade on and based in The Netherlands, she is the owner of her own thriving Internet retail business, The Needlework Boutique, selling cross–stitch supplies both online and at various consumer craft shows. For Bernadette, this was an obvious choice.

'I have a very strong personal interest in needlework,' she says, 'and I couldn't get what I wanted locally.' Sick of always complaining about not having the supplies available and always having to get them shipped in from the United States, Bernadette set about solving the problem by creating her own business.

Although Bernadette admits to having absolutely no professional experience when it comes to running a business, she does believe that her former guises as a teacher and student have afforded her some of the necessary attributes.

'My background means that I am always confident in researching what I need to know,' she says. Coupled with this, Bernadette is also a self–confessed perfectionist, interested in constantly learning new things and meeting new people. Despite her lack of experience in the entrepreneurial world however, it was only a matter of six months and an initial investment of around €3,000 before Bernadette was up and running, although, she admits that she feels she still has a long way to go.

Initially, Bernadette started out offering her needlework wares online only, but quickly realised that she needed a personal presence, so arranged to have regular open days in a classroom at a local quilt shop. After a period of time, this fell through, as the owner of the quilt shop required the classrooms for classes. It was at that point that Bernadette branched out into attending carefully selected retail shows, many of which she conducted in Dutch, and which have proved quite successful.

Creating The Needlework Boutique has proved to be one long lesson that Bernadette has learned along the way.

'There are various new skills I have had to pick up,' she says, 'such as website building, accounts and marketing.' But perhaps the biggest lesson has been the pivotal role that networking plays in creating any thriving business. In the past, I marketed the business mainly by advertising in magazines, but that didn't work and proved to be an expensive marketing attempt.' Now Bernadette attends regular networking groups, such as Connecting Women, based in The Hague, and communicates online with other needleworkers in news lists and other online forums.

'Although I do generate new customers through word–of–mouth, networking is extremely important,' she enthuses. 'Not only can you get new customers, but you can also find appropriate solutions for your own needs. Successful networking is really just a question of confidence – something I am still developing.'

As a mother of three, to 8 year–old Alex, 6 year–old Shannon and 2 year–old Stephanie, Bernadette finds that the business fits in particularly well with her situation.

'I do most of my work at a desk in a small corner of the house right next to the gas heater for the central heating and hot water,' she explains. 'I spend most of the daytime looking after my youngest and I spend about one and a half hours at the computer, marketing, reading emails, doing my accounts and packaging orders. After the children are in bed, I try to spend another couple of hours on the computer or on other business needs.'

Bernadette soon intends to relocate back to Australia, taking The Needlework Boutique with her; something which shouldn't prove too problematic since the major source of her income is via the Internet.

Excited by the prospect of returning to her native land, Bernadette is also pleased that she made the initial move to The Netherlands.

'If I had never come overseas, I would be still teaching,' she says. 'I'd be content, but not as happy as I am now. I may have been richer in money, but not in spirit.' Having said that, if you are looking to set up your own business, Bernadette warns that you must be sure it is what you want.

'Many people who enter business experience burnout after about five years,' she advises. 'Also, be aware that the money isn't everything. You will probably never get rich doing this. In the needlework industry, the type of money you make really depends on the person doing the job and what exactly they are doing. Many store owners are able to raise a family on the strength of what they earn in the shop, it just depends on the product mix and the person.'

'Always research the idea carefully,' says Bernadette, 'if you choose to go it alone, be sure that you are strong enough to keep reinventing yourself and your company. And always be aware of your limitations; if you can't do something, then employ someone who can. I always use a Dutch accountant because I know that my Dutch is too poor for me to follow the tax information properly.'

A fine example of an expatriate who has made a business out of a problem, Bernadette has successfully created a portable career out of her favourite hobby.

BERNADETTE WOULD LIKE TO SHARE THE FOLLOWING

You can contact Bernadette on: info@needleworkboutique.com

For more information on her Internet retail business, visit: www.needleworkboutique.com

Websites

Guerilla Marketing: www.gmarketing.com

Mompreneurs Online: www.mompreneursonline.com

Books

Cobe, P and Parlapiano, E.H *Mompreneurs*, Doubleday Books

Edwards, P and Edwards, S *Making Money with your Computer at Home*, Jeremy P Tarcher

Jay Conrad Levinson, et al, *Guerilla Marketing for the Home–Based Business*, Houghton Mifflin

Parfitt, J *Career in Your Suitcase 2*, Lean Marketing Press

Bernadette's Tips

Acknowledge your weaknesses and find a solution to them.

Stay positive at all times

Plan well. As some experts say, 'luck is what happens when preparation meets opportunity.'

PAUL AND JULIA HERBERT

Key Information

A career in Website Management, Development and Design

Age: 52 & 51

Nationality: British

Status: Married with 3 children

Countries lived in: UK, Germany, Cyprus and France

Qualifications: None. But as Paul says so eloquently: 'I was expelled from two schools and left school at 15. I think I got an O level in religious instruction, which has come in very handy for an Atheist.' Julia was an army child and went to 26 schools, she failed religious instruction. 'My last headmaster told me on leaving, "Herbert you are going to walk out of these gates and fall flat on your face." He was right and it was the only piece of information that he imparted that was of any use. The only thing that has set me apart from all the other kids who have fallen flat on their face after leaving school is my ability to keep getting up. Neither of us have a qualification between us but I have always found that qualities not qualifications are needed to ensure success.'

Years on the move: 12

Paul and Julia Herbert and their three children, Samantha, eight, Jay, six and Ryan, three were forced to move to their dilapidated French farmhouse in The Dordogne in 1995. Paul had lost almost everything the family owned through litigation with a former employer, which went horribly wrong.

They arrived in France to find rain pouring

through the ceiling and with only a few hundred pounds to their name.

'I can remember arriving just before midnight, my children crying that they wanted to go home. It's not easy explaining to a three year old who has been used to a large, luxurious house, that his new home is run down and smelly, and where the only running water is that which is coming in through the roof,' recalls Paul.

The first summer the Herberts eked out some kind of living selling the €2000.00 of children's clothes they had taken with them to sell at a local market. When the tourists went home, their market dried up.

Not to be deterred they decided that no job was beneath them and for the next few years they would garden, clean, do odd–jobs, fell trees, paint, decorate and undertake any menial work that came their way. Neighbours gave them vegetables and eggs, and, thanks to a pair of walnut trees, the family became accustomed to walnut omelettes. Despite great difficulties the family never gave up.

Over time Paul and Julia found through personal experience and feedback from friends that it was difficult to get accurate and up to date information about rental holiday accommodation in France. They learned that 80% of calls people made to enquire about accommodation availability were a waste of time both for the potential holiday maker and the owner, as they were usually booked in peak periods. With this in mind they developed an idea that would provide a solution to the problem and change their family's fortune.

They decided to set up a centralised booking system that would operate via the Internet and www.franceonecall.com was born. The site specialises in listing self– catering accommodation of all styles from gîtes and villas to apartments in every region in France.

With a background in Sales and Marketing, gained from working for a Life Assurance company in the UK, Paul had the essential skill of cold calling potential clients when he set up his new website business. It was an invaluable skill, as the inbuilt discipline of contacting clients helped the business to succeed. He also says that as an ex life assurance salesman 'no one has endurance like the man who sells insurance.'

Via the website the holiday maker can quickly and easily find lists of possible accommodation either by travel date or region. It is then only a matter of seconds until availability is confirmed. France One Call is proud to provide information on more holiday properties in France than anyone else.

Properties on the database are monitored for its standard via feedback from the people who have visited it. Accommodation is also awarded a globe rating for quality, which helps the holiday maker to book a holiday with confidence.

So what makes this entrepreneur special? Paul's skill lies in being able to recognise related areas, exploit any opportunities and expand them into successful businesses. Now England, Spain, Portugal, Italy and America are all represented in this same way with websites using the recognisable brand name Onecall.

France One Call is now part of the larger WhereOnEarthGroup (www.whereonearthgroup.com) aimed at people who are interested in holidaying or living abroad and offers a range of support services.

Advice to would–be website owners from Paul is for them to understand the Internet and how it works. It is imperative to learn why one website succeeds where another fails.

'It doesn't matter how stunning the website looks, if the search engines don't like the way it's constructed, the website won't be highly ranked by the major search engines,' he says. It is also vital to research your market, check out the viability of your idea and its competition before pricing or product at the right level for that market. 'Do your homework,' he continues

In order to stay ahead of the game Paul and Julia have had to become experts about every area of their business.

'I have made it my personal mission to understand everything I can about the Internet and the search engines,' says Paul. This came about via trial and error and the eventual realisation that they couldn't trust other companies to get the results they wanted.

But their ambitions did not stop there and the Where on Earth group was set up in 2000. This company was established because they now owned, had acquired or merged a number of companies that, though related, operated in different areas. And the group had become unwieldy. So, the network of IT companies, the One Call companies and all their related websites for property sales worldwide, car rentals, removals, insurance and other related services came under review.

In truth, the initial One Call operation had suffered from several costly errors. One of the Directors had embezzled money, and a general lack of experience in the field meant that a lot of money was spent on companies who promised to deliver services, but which did not. However, despite these setbacks Paul was always optimistic and able to see the positive side of any situation he was in.

It seems as if they never stop having ideas and when they do Paul hands them over to his team who turn them into business systems.

The result was that Paul, Julia and Leo Ossewijer, a Dutch Director of one of the companies, bought out most of the other Directors of the One Call group, turning a bad situation to their advantage. This provided more control, and by setting up www.whereonearthgroup.com the company as a whole was streamlined and made more efficient through the shared use of technology and information. The group is privately owned, with its HQ in London, and is backed by Eldershot Capital Partners, MJ Technologies and Reuters Venture Capital.

Where on Earth is a technology company that combines innovative algorithms with global information about specific locations. They have clients such as The Marriott and Royal and Sun Alliance. The group combines different activities: online search and advertising, risk assessment for companies and wireless location based services.

Different applications have been developed for each area and client. Clients are able to link specific information related to their industry to specific locations to enable them to make knowledgeable and factual business decisions.

The notion of location is central to the concept of the Where on Earth group. Its aim is to 'put location on the Internet,' says Paul. When they learned that web searches are the second most common use of the Internet after email it was a natural progression for the group to develop solutions to the problem of how to optimise web searches for both companies and the individual.

The Where on Earth team members are now based all over the world, but still form a successful and cohesive whole.

'I have been lucky in employing some very clever IT people. We encourage free thinking within the group so that the business develops in all areas,' continues Paul.

Based in the Dordogne, the French team consists of Julia Herbert, who is Managing Director, Leo Ossewijer, Head of IT, Paul Herbert, Head of Business Development, Lesley Roads, Managing Director of Tour Operations and Alexander Rawlings, Design and IT support. There are also other team members based in England, Spain and Malta and various other associates and affiliates (which include car hire, removals, holidays, insurance and so on) based in many different locations.

Everyone on the team has a financial interest in their side of the business. They also have an interest in the success of every aspect of the business. In this way motivation and involvement is kept at a peak, Paul explains.

The range of activities covered by the Where on Earth group reflects the pro–active approach taken to building the business, finding solutions and putting them into practice. Every service they provide is related and of course you can find a full explanation of these on the website.

The Where on Earth group is now recognised as one of the leaders in Internet optimisation and is uniquely placed to enable anyone who wants to set up an Internet business anywhere in the world to get launched. Paul is proud to claim that he believes that no–one else has the infrastructure to be able to achieve what they do. They never stop being flexible and are determined to find workable solutions for their clients.

New business is acquired, and the company marketed too via search engines, linking strategies and word of mouth. The business is not advertised through standard print media at all, as they believe they would be merely wasting time talking to people they would never do business with. Their success at website optimisation means they can ensure that their own website is always found by those who are looking for them. Business is so good in their new website design company that they have a three month waiting list of new clients.

Clearly the company is in a constant state of growth, and is continually developing new ideas and services. So, in some respects it is difficult to say exactly what the future holds for Paul and Julia. They talk about floating the company by 2010.

'My biggest frustration is the speed we are able to put ideas into practice,' says Paul.

Motivation for the whole team comes from the sheer pace of development and change in the company, the constant flow of ideas brings endless new business opportunities their way. At any given time there can be between 20 and 30 ongoing projects, so no–one has time to get bored or complacent.

Family support has been vital to their success and remained one of the constant factors for them during times that were turbulent, difficult and full of change. It was also important that their children were young enough at eight, six and three that their education was not severely affected by the move. They have grown up into mature, bilingual young adults, state Paul and Julia proudly.

When asked why they were successful when others with far greater bank balances or experience may have failed, Paul said that, 'the difference between success and failure is the ability to get up and keep getting up, and to keep trying until you find a workable solution.' You can see from their story that they did just that and achieved enormous success and personal growth along the way.

PAUL WOULD LIKE TO SHARE THE FOLLOWING

You can contact Paul directly on tel: 0033 (0)553916544

He is happy to talk to anyone who has questions, and says if he doesn't know the answer he will know someone who does!

You can email Paul at: paul@franceonecall.com

Where On Earth Group: www.whereonearthgroup.com

Websites

Bonjour magazine: www.bonjourmagazine.com

One Call Estates: www.onecallestates.com

Well Earned Breaks: www.wellearnedbreaks.com

France Review: www.francereview.com

Europe's leading travel network: www.holiday–web–sites.com

Scopula Website design: www.scopula.com

Paul and Julia's Tips

Make sure you speak to a set number of prospective clients everyday. Don't let anything distract you from this.

Invest in a good, correctly optimised Internet site. Don't use a best friend to design it and make sure you are offering something innovative and unique.

Do your research. Make sure there is a market for your product or service.

YVONNE QUAHE COLIN–JONES

Key Information

Career Counsellor and Inter–Cultural Trainer who is a partner in a management consultancy

Age: Fifty something

Nationality: Singaporean

Status: Married to Graham (British) with two children.

Countries lived in: United Kingdom, Hong Kong, Singapore, Philippines, USA

Qualifications: BA Hons Sociology – University of Sussex, licensed practitioner Myers–Briggs Type Inventory (Oxford Psychologists), Training and Development (Ateneo de Manila Philippines)

Years on the move: 25

When Yvonne returned to her native Singapore with her British husband, this time as an expatriate spouse, she was excited about being home again and able to do as she pleased having no work permit restrictions and a wealth of employment opportunities before her. Then she discovered that, as a Singaporean, she would have to work on local terms. Local terms included just 14 days annual leave, while her husband had 42 days leave. The family wanted to travel and so Yvonne, devastated, booked to see a career counsellor.

'That was the best $100 I've spent in my life,' she says. 'When the counsellor knew that I was likely to continue to be mobile she discussed the issue of developing a portable career. Since then I have always had the concept of a 'portable career' in mind.'

Yvonne believes that a portable career allows you to develop entrepreneurial qualities while retaining the flexibility to explore and be free during school holidays.

The family moved to Manila, and it was there that Yvonne became a partner in a small management consultancy, Transitions Asia, which is also the alliance partner of Ricklin–Echikson Associates for whom Yvonne also worked as an expatriate consultant. She specialised in cross–cultural training, with emphasis on cross cultural team–building, pre–departure preparation, relocation, writing materials, developing intranets and handbooks for companies on living in Manila, spouse employment and third culture children.

Her work led her to become involved in assisting accompanying partners with their transition and to explore traditional and non–traditional career options. Since some countries will not employ non–nationals, it is important to find innovative ways to help spouses/partners enhance their international knowledge and remain productive.

'The success of Transitions Asia is based on its emphasis in helping clients understand Filipino values and how they impact on behaviour so that the expatriate can ascribe correct meanings to the behaviour they encounter, both personally and professionally,' she explains.

Having a portable career has provided Yvonne with the opportunities to make friendships with host country nationals. She has particularly enjoyed working with Filipino colleagues and developing an understanding of another culture and its people.

She feels this has helped her maintain equilibrium in a transient community.

However she feels strongly that we must learn to understand the separation between satisfaction and remuneration. These may not come in tandem because in certain countries the wage structure is far lower than that of our home countries. She believes that finding your passion is the only true solution.

'Look on the bright side,' she says. 'The person with the 'second career' has the luxury of choice. If you are not responsible for putting the bread on the table you can choose the work that you enjoy.'

In summer 2002 Yvonne moved back to England so as to be nearer her children who had started school in the UK. Yvonne admits repatriation has been 'extremely difficult' as many UK employers do not really value overseas experience. Yvonne first worked for School Choice International, which provides school search consultancy to international families, as well as offering freelance business briefings. She then moved to work with 4 Square Relocation and was an account manager for Sony. During this time, she was in charge of orchestrating the group move of 128 families over a period of just four months. At one point she had to organise 17 home finding visits and 13 check–ins. In both of these jobs she has been able to utilise and call on her own experience as an expatriate.

In October 2005 the family moved on again, this time to Washington DC, where they are looking forward very much to a new challenge.

YVONNE WOULD LIKE TO SHARE THE FOLLOWING

You can contact Yvonne on: Colinjones888@hotmail.com

Books

Stewart, T.A *Intellectual Capital* Nicholas Brealey Publishing

Invaluable tool in helping you understand your host culture.

Conferences

Global Living: www.globalliving.org

Families in Global Transition: www.figt.org

Women's International Networking Conference: www.winconference.net

Websites

ExpatExpert: www.expatexpert.com

Ricklin–Echikson Associates: www.r–e–a.com

Yvonne's Tips

Take time to understand the culture of the country you are going to as it will help you understand your hosts/host country.

Know yourself and your needs/reactions during times of stress and transition.

Make an effort to continue your career, even 'seemingly useless detours' may turn out to be doors of opportunity.

Maintain a sense of humour – nothing is forever.

ALISON DOLAN

Key Information

A career in network marketing

Age: 52

Nationality: British

Status: Married 17 years

Countries lived in: Greece, Germany, Sicily, USA and Spain since 1988

Qualifications: A levels

Years on the move: 32

Promoting products instore and working as a financial consultant for the Automobile Association with responsibility for the whole of the north of England proved to be the perfect training ground for Alison Dolan, who, since moving to Spain in 1988 now sells wellness products for a vast international company called Nikken. Alison is so successful that she has become a Platinum Distributor and has now earned her second car through the bonuses she has earned. This time it is an Audi TT.

Network marketing, or Multi Level Marketing, as it is also called, has gained an unfair reputation, and is often referred to as 'pyramid selling'. Few MLM companies still operate on this basis and Nikken is certainly not one of them. In fact, this kind of business may offer the perfect solution to anyone looking to start a new career overseas with little capital. For while new distributors have to buy a small amount of products and marketing materials to start with, the commission earned can be high. This can be the perfect business for anyone who likes meeting people and finds networking easy.

People do business with people who like them, and networking is simply about making friends. For Alison, this has posed no problem at all.

'I have lots of experience of communicating with people, understanding needs and trying to find the right solutions for them,' she says. 'I am a good networker. I have joined the Women in Business group in Marbella and I network everywhere I go with anyone who is willing to talk to me.' As a result almost all of Alison's clients come to her via word of mouth referral.

But things were not always so easy for Alison. Five years after she arrived in Spain, Alison was struck down with Chronic Fatigue Syndrome, which lasted for a further five years. And it was then, by complete chance that Nikken came into her life and changed it forever.

'I had tried about every cure known to man by then and none were effective for long. My husband, James, who runs his own expat financial services business, was visiting a friend who lives nearby and brought back some information about magnetic insoles. Eventually, I managed to track the product down and after two days of wearing them I had unbelievable energy out of the blue and felt fantastic! My health took a dramatic upturn so much so that we felt we wanted to know everything we could about how this had worked and what the company was all about. The more we researched it the more it made sense and I became a distributor in 1999.'

When you become a distributor for a network marketing company it is not quite like buying a franchise where you pay for a business model and training and then work for yourself. With MLM you are recruited by an existing distributor, who becomes your 'upline'. Alison's upline lives in Leicester in England. Once you are a distributor you are responsible for promoting and selling products and also for recruiting more distributors who in turn become your 'downline'. The more people you have working for you, the more bonuses you can earn from the sales made by them. In this way you really can make money without doing anything yourself. The most successful distributors give regular training, coaching and motivation to their teams in order to keep them keen and effective.

Alison has hundreds of people in her downline now but it is only the people who work consistently who make a real difference to Alison's own business. There are relatively few star performers, but those who have potential are worth nurturing.

'I have people working in Norway, Switzerland, Portugal and Spain who are serious business builders,' continues Alison. 'I think you need to have six people in your downline with a vision to succeed in order to make it to the top. Those people will go out and replicate what they do. So look for six freedom–minded people and you are away. People can be fickle and difficult, often saying one thing and meaning another. I have learned to let go of the outcome and not get emotionally attached to it.'

'I train and coach my downline. For many people this business is very different from anything they have done before, in fact, even if someone has been in MLM before they have no experience of Nikken so they need training and support in the products as well as how to create a successful business,' she says.

Any distributor, at any level, is entitled to take part in a wide range of superb personal and business development training seminars held in Milton Keynes in the UK or to attend any locally held meetings. The company cannot be accused of taking your money and leaving you to it. In fact the money you need to start up can be as little as you like and Nikken never encourage anyone to stretch themselves financially at the outset. Alison spent more than many as her original investment was for £5,000 worth of products.

Alison continues to be motivated by her own success and the success of her downline, but more importantly perhaps, she continues to be passionate about the products. To be successful in this field it is vital that you truly believe in the product you sell and that you use it yourself. This is a business where it pays to be authentic. Alison now uses everything Nikken produces. The company is perhaps best known for its range of magnetic or far–infrared products, such as insoles, jackets, jewellery and pain relieving supports, which work by increasing blood circulation and speeding up the healing process. But the company also produces a range of sleep systems, duvets, mattresses and pillows as well as make up, face creams, training shoes and even water filter and oxygenation systems. Like most companies of this type, they are always coming up with new products.

'The products are designed to help you create a healthy 'wellness' lifestyle without it taking hours every day. They can be used while you are sitting, walking or sleeping and you can wear them too. You can also benefit from them as nutritional supplementation and the use of pure living water. In short, we can create 'wellness' homes where we can nurture and protect our health by using natural products that cannot harm but only help us to maintain our health,' she explains.

Her typical week is spent balancing the need to keep in touch with existing distributors and to support their efforts while constantly staying alert to new opportunities to sell products and recruit. She is also determined to balance her work commitments with her family, and her youngest daughter, Sophie, still lives at home.

'I refuse to take phone calls between six and eight pm so that we can have a meal together and I can help with homework,' she says. 'And I have always put important family or school events into my diary. However, I have travelled a great deal too and my husband has been my greatest support.'

The Daltons and their three children, Fiona, 27, Joshua, 16 and Sophie, 15, call the 'white village' of Jimena de la Frontera in the province of Cadiz in Andalucia, home. They are about 25 minutes from the Mediterranean and 40 minutes from Gibraltar, They own 13 acres of land and have a beautiful ranch style house with stunning views of the Moorish town and surrounding mountains as well as the National Park. Both Alison and James work from offices in their home. Alison thinks that there must be about 200 other expats in her village, but most of them just own holiday homes.

'As I live close to a very cosmopolitan coast here in Spain, I thought it would be a great opportunity to access other expats who may be interested in living abroad but create a business via their contacts back home. This has worked quite well and I have never stopped talking to anyone, anywhere about what I do and who I am looking for. Wherever you are where there are people you can softly and gently introduce your business. I never push anyone or make them feel that I am selling. I want them to be curious enough to want to sit down with me and talk through my business on a one to one basis. I believe that everyone knows someone who could be interested and that it is simply a sifting process.'

Alison's positive attitude about her work and her determination to stay on the look out for opportunities at all time, coupled with her passion for products she believes in one hundred per cent are clearly behind her huge success.

ALISON WOULD LIKE TO SHARE THE FOLLOWING

You can contact Alison on: healthiswealth@terra.es

Websites

Nikken: www.nikkenuk.com or www.nikken.com

Books

Hill, N *Think and Grow Rich*, Jeremy P Tarcher

Kiyosaki, R.T *Rich Dad Poor Dad*, Time Warner Paperbacks

Kiyosaki, R.T *The Cashflow Quadrant*, TechPress

Kalench, J *Being the Best you Can Be in MLM*, Atlantic Books

Ludbrook, E *The Big Picture*, Legacy Communications

Berry, R *Direct Selling*, Butterworth–Heinemann

Yarnell, M Power Multi–Level Marketing, Atlantic Books

Carmichael, A Network and *Multi–Level Marketing*, Concept

Organisations

Women in Business in Marbella: www.wibspain.com

Other MLM companies

Forever–Living (aloe vera products): www.forever–living.com

Weekenders (uncrushable clothes): www.weekenders.com

Mary Kay (make up): www.marykay.com

Likisma (aromatherapy products): www.likisma–aroma.co.uk

Amway (for hundreds of products): www.amway.com

Tupperware (plastic and kitchen ware): www.tupperware.com

Avon Cosmetics (make up and toiletries): www.avon.com

Ann Summers (lingerie and bedtime recreation): www.annsummers.com

Usborne Books at Home: www.usbournebooksathome.co.uk

Alison's Tips

Be clear on where you are going and most importantly, why you want it.

Make a commitment to stick to it for at least three years.

Be open to taking advice and stick close to and listen to someone in your upline who is gaining the success you are looking for – better to follow someone through a minefield that to think you know it all and to strike out on your own.

JACINTA NOONAN

Key Information

A career as a corporate and life coach and trainer to companies and individuals

Age: 44

Nationality: Australian

Status: Married to a Dutchman

Countries lived in: United States of America, Australia and Netherlands

Qualifications: Diploma in Teaching (Primary), Bachelor of Science Hons (Psychology), NLP Master Practitioner, Certified Coach, Certificates in Eating Disorders, Essential Obesity, Certification in Advanced Facilitation / Deep Democracy, Leadership: Strengthening Influence & Impact, Citation in Entrepreneurship

Years on the move: 20

When Jacinta Noonan arrived in The Netherlands to attend a friend's wedding 16 years ago, she had no idea that she would end up staying here, marrying a Dutchman and running her own executive coaching and training business. Back then, she had been making her living as a primary school teacher in Australia. But when, like Jacinta, you are the kind of person who sniffs out opportunities and grabs them with both hands, life's path can be something of a zigzag.

'I started off working at a blue–chip technology company, as an inventory control co–ordinator. It had nothing to do with my training or experience and I spent my days doing data input and analysis,' she says.

'A year later I found something that was much more up my street, and though I started off as a Teacher of English as a Foreign Language (TEFL) ended up managing the English teaching department for an executive language institute in Amsterdam. Here I was responsible for developing and implementing customised training programs some of which were residential. This was a really wide–ranging job and I had to do everything from project management to recruitment and training the trainers.'

After more than four years, and having had enough of the low pay that can be associated with TEFL teaching, Jacinta tripled her income by moving to an international pharmaceutical company. Here she assumed responsibility for developing and running a range of workshops mostly associated with sales. Now she was training all over the world and though the work was interesting, Jacinta ended up spending about four hours a day in a traffic jam.

'My choices were to leave the company or move to the South of Holland. Instead I decided to form my own company, which is called Soulworks, and fulfil my dream of working for myself.'

Jacinta wanted to be a coach and swap the classroom for engaging one–to–one with clients. To kick off, she took a coaches' training course with International Training Seminars, which was excellent.

'I did all my training with ITS,' says Jacinta. 'First I did NLP, I liked the values of Ian McDermott and the course was sensational and the training perfect so I decided to continue with ITS.'

Each course consisted of 20 days face–to–face training over a period of five months, taken at four intense days once a month with practise in between. In fact you cannot apply for the coaching training until you have completed the NLP Practitioner Course and followed by the NLP Master Practitioner course. They cost her about £2,500 each.

Setting up a business was relatively easy. She signed up with the Kamer van Koophandel, or Chamber of Commerce and the Belastingdienst, tax office and was away.

'Of course I also had to open a bank account, start doing VAT, get a website, a logo, a brand a letterhead and purchase my office equipment, but it was relatively easy. I had gained many skills in my previous corporate work and knew about project management and administration. I'm so glad I had that experience behind me. And of course, training is still very much part of my core business.'

Her new line of work allowed her to focus on the results, challenges and changes that her clients may need to make. After a few sessions she watches her clients become more valuable to themselves or to their employers.

Despite her success Jacinta knows that this is a competitive market, with coaches being ten a penny these days. Recognising that one to one coaching alone may not pay the bills she decided to devise and offer a range of training programs too and again she could rely on her teaching skills.

Today, Soulworks runs a number of inspirational and unique programs, all focusing on helping other people to get the most out of life and be the best they can. Her coaching clients tend to be both expatriate and Dutch and from all walks of life with many in their 30s and 40s. She still runs Presenting Powerfully and Exhibition Stand Crew Training as she did for her old company but has now added Negotiating in English and Find Your Passion to her portfolio. But it is perhaps her Big on the Inside program that illustrates her creativity at its best.

'The program is designed to help individuals to reach their fullest potential,' she says. 'I call it Big on the Inside, because many people, women particularly, hamper their own success because they feel their body is the wrong shape. I help my clients to be big on the inside, where it matters and to lose their hang–ups about external appearance once and for all.'

Big on the Inside offers workshops, individual coaching and support groups and Jacinta is developing a range of products to help people in their quest to reach their potential. In November 2004, she published her first book, called *'My Perfect Weight'*.

'Being the author of a book has improved my reputation,' says Jacinta. 'And, of course, I make money from it too as many of my students and clients buy a copy after working with me.'

Jacinta is a fine example of someone who is big on the inside. The skills and experience she has acquired along the way are not inconsiderable. In addition to the general administration and management side of things she has taught herself to create and manage her own websites and looks after www.bigontheinside.com and www.soulworks.nl completely alone. She also now takes marketing, printing and production, sales and using a wide range of computer programs in her stride.

'My goodness, the learning curve is massive. I never knew anything about digital printing versus lithographic or finances, government expectations and tax before this!'

Marketing, of course, is key to the success of the business and Jacinta is a believer in the power of networking as a tool to growing her client base.

'Networking is very effective. You get yourself known to many people and, let's face it, people prefer to buy from people who have been referred to them or that they have met personally,' she explains. Jacinta belongs to two active professional women's organisations in Holland and is a board member for both. She belongs to Connecting Women (www.connectingwomen.nl) in The Hague and Women's International Network (WIN) in Amsterdam (www.womensinternational.net).

'I like meeting incredibly diverse women at the meetings. I also have a pool of knowledge that I can tap into. For example, I got advice from a woman at WIN about the pitfalls of starting a business partnership. If I need a lawyer, I can access someone in the network and it is a good way to make friends – that is if you are not too shy to push yourself forwards, often, at times when you don't feel like it.'

Through her involvement with WIN she has her name put forward for a number of projects and has found individual coaching clients and students at both clubs. She is the VP of Member Relations at WIN and Vice–Chair at Connecting Women.

'I highly advise that people join the board, particularly if they are shy. I always have something to do at meetings, and having to welcome newcomers and stand in for the Chair now and again is actually easier than being just one of the crowd.'

In addition to her monthly networking and board meetings, Jacinta markets her business by producing some beautiful flyers, which she distributes to a number of other clubs and associations and English bookshops that are frequented by her target market. She also advertises in as many expatriate magazines and websites as she can find. In fact many of her clients come to her from the Elynx website (www.elynx.nl).

'I find the biggest challenge is to target my advertising budget to the right places, but have learned to monitor where everyone comes from so that I can market as wisely as possible.'

In the four years since she started Soulworks, Jacinta has found that she needs to keep abreast of new markets and constantly tweak and hone her courses to fit emerging needs and trends. And while the workshops can be both satisfying and lucrative the amount of organisation she needs to do is relatively time consuming. However, many of the students who attend the workshops ultimately turn to her for one–to–one coaching, and so her aim is to get as much repeat business and referral as possible.

'The coaching business was pretty quick to get up and running, and to conduct the training I just needed a nice room in my house for the clients who come to me. I go to the offices of my corporate clients and I talk to many clients on the telephone, so this is pretty flexible. Fee rates vary considerably, and competition is stiff as more and more people turn to a coaching profession precisely because of this flexibility. Some people charge as little at €30 and hour, while others charge €500 or more depending on their experience and specialisms.'

Jacinta is glad that she has a number of income streams, allowing her great variety and keeping her open to more opportunities. Some months she can have several days' training for a corporate client, others she focuses on running her own workshops for individuals, or on her writing.

'Think carefully before becoming a life coach,' she cautions. 'To make a living in this one field is not easy. If you are extremely good at selling yourself and have lots of corporate work too you will succeed. Otherwise it can be hard to get enough consistent clients to pay the bills. Coaching can be taken anywhere in the world, but having more than one string to your bow is crucial.'

They often say that we end up teaching what we need to learn ourselves and Jacinta's own life lessons have come to her by running her Find Your Passion workshops.

'If you are to stay motivated by your work you must do something that you love and that means that you cannot ignore some of the facets of your personality thinking that they are not relevant or important,' she says. 'I have always loved music. I sing, I play the guitar and I the piano. Music is like a constant itch and I have to have it in my life or I do not feel whole. I recently found a way to include my passion in my workshops and now sing and play as part of the program. Now that I am comfortable being my authentic self at work as well as at play people get to know the real me, my work has had a big injection of energy and it is really paying off. No–one can train in the style of someone else. It won't work. You have to be yourself and use your own stories as illustrations. I have to walk my talk. How could I run a Find Your Passion course if I did not think I had found my own and were really using it in the workplace?'

Working from home means that four hour daily commutes are a thing of the past, though she now finds that her office contents have a habit of spilling into the rest of the house and it's easy to slip into the habit of dressing too casually. It can also get lonely.

'I feel that a team of people around you is essential if you work alone. Other people can stimulate, support and motivate you, give you a reality check, perspective and be there for brainstorming. They are also a rich resource of skills, contacts and ideas,' she says, and it is for this reason that she makes time to meet with other solopreneurs as often as she can and tries to work alongside other people with some of her projects.

JACINTA WOULD LIKE TO SHARE THE FOLLOWING

You can contact Jacinta on: j.noonan@soulworks.nl

Websites

Big on the Inside: www.bigontheinside.com

Soulworks: www.soulworks.nl

Chamber of Commerce (Kamer van Koophandel): www.kvk.nl

Tax Office (Belastingdienst): www.belastingdienst.nl

Tips on cold calling: www.wendyweiss.com

Tips on authentic marketing: www.mollygordon.com

Sell without pressure: www.unlockthegame.com

For newsletters and autoresponders and merchant accounts: www.1shoppingcart.com

Online payment tool: www.paypal.com

Free software: www.openoffice.org

Advertise events in the Netherlands: www.elynx.nl and www.webfoot.nl

Books

Noonan, J *My Perfect Weight*, www.bigontheinside.com

Gerber, M *The E–Myth Revisited*, Harper Collins

Sher, B, Gottlieb, A *Wishcraft: How to get What you Really Want*, Ballantine Books

Franks, L *The Seed Handboo: The Feminine Way to Create Business*, Piatkus Books

McKenna, P *Change Your Life in Seven Days*, Bantam Press

Adams, MG PhD *Change your Questions, Change your Life*, Berrett–Koehler

Hawes, M, Baker, J *Coach Yourself to Wealth*, Allen & Unwin

Souza, B *Become Who you Were Born to Be*, Paragon Holdings

Coaching Books

Zeus, P and Skiffington, S *The Complete Guide to Coaching at Work*, McGraw Hill

Zeus, P and Skiffington, S *The Coaching At Work Toolkit*, McGraw Hill Publishing Co.

Whitworth, J et al *Co–Active Coaching*, Davies–Black Publishing

O'Neill, M.B *Executive Coaching with Backbone and Heart*, Jossey–Bass Wiley

Gallwey, W.T *The Inner Game of Tennis*, Pan

Gallwey, W.T *The Inner Game of Work*, Texere Publishing

Whitmore, J *Coaching for Performance*, Nicholas Brealey Publishing

Organisations

International Training Seminars: www.itsnlp.com

Connecting women: www.connectingwomen.nl

Women's International Network: www.womensinternational.net

Improve your speaking: www.toastmasters.com

Amsterdam American Business Club: www.aabc.nl

Jacinta's Tips

Believe in yourself and what you are worth.

Be open to and follow up the opportunities that are presented.

Get the right information from the people who really know, not from people who aren't the experts!

JO AND JOHN STURGES

Key Information

Running a bed and breakfast and two villas in France

Age: 59 and 58 respectively

Nationality: British

Status: Married with grow–up children

Countries lived in: UK and France

Qualifications: Degree in Publishing / BA in Economics

Years on the move: 2

With the demands of running a busy pub in Essex, John and Jo knew they wanted something similar, but with less pressure . . . and hopefully better weather.

Having been travelling to France since 1959, Jo and John knew France offered the better weather, less initial outlay and a good tourist demand. Their idea of opening a Bed and Breakfast establishment in France was born.

'We knew we enjoyed providing a service to people, as well as enjoying their company so we saw this as an opportunity to have a better quality of life whilst generating an income,' says Jo.

Knowing they needed an income quickly, Jo and John decided to purchase an existing business in the Dordogne area of France. They had looked for properties in various areas of France, but once they had seen this property, they fell for it straight away.

'It is a little out of the touristy area, situated near Sarlat and Montignac. There are still plenty of tourists but the pace is gentler and this area gives a real taste of rural France. We purchased our house and two guesthouses, one sleeping up to eight people and the other sleeping up to 12', explains Jo. 'We had only six weeks before our first guests arrived. As the properties were rundown, these were the hardest six weeks of our lives!' she continues.

Both Jo and John speak some French and read it quite well, but explained how amazing they find it that many people move to France with virtually no knowledge of the language and still manage perfectly well.

They get on fine with the locals, who they described as pleasant and friendly, and they try to attend as many as possible of the functions organised by them, even the local Bingo.

'Living in France is brilliant and the better weather certainly benefits us a lot,' says John. 'Some of the sacrosanct French traditions, such as lunchtime closing, are dying out and the emergence of the 'fast–food culture' is taking a grip.'

They joined France's Micro–Enterprise tax system as it is the simplest and does not require you to submit annual accounts.

'The French authorities assume your running costs to be approximately 70% of your income and only tax you on the remaining 30%,' explains John. 'This works up to a certain point,' says Jo, 'but you can never get rich under this regime.'

Restrictions and challenges have also included the need to take out extensive insurance, including public liability.

'We had an electricity check for our own peace of mind more than anything, but had to meet the legal requirements of having our chimneys swept and fencing the swimming pool before we could open to our first guests.'

Now running a large property with two separate houses, both with swimming pools, they remain continually surprised by how much equipment is required. They have huge supplies of linen, cleaning materials, a startling collection of tools, lawnmowers and tractors not to mention about 20 bicycles to suit every age and ability of guest.

Their initial set–up costs were considerable and more than expected. Apart from the initial property purchase, they incurred expenses of at least an additional £10,000.

In theory you can earn a very good living running two villas and a bed and breakfast business, but this is dependant on the type of property you can afford. The larger and better presented it is the more you can earn, although running expenses can be higher. Also worth noting is that the law is subject to change, sometimes resulting in major unexpected costs. France is seasonal so your choice of area is important too. The mountain areas might give two seasons, whereas the hotter spots might attract people seeking winter warmth.

'If you can generate an annual income of £25,000 you are doing very well,' says Jo.

Now established, Jo and John relish the challenge of giving their guests a great holiday. They strive to meet their guests' specific requirements and are relaxed about other people's different needs and behaviours.

They rate the best things about their job as being the variety of work and meeting new people all the time. For John especially, the best thing is being his own boss (well, 'nearly', says Jo).

'The hardest things are the constant pressure on the houses from the weather, along with the wear and tear on furnishings from rather heavy–handed people!' says John.

Their typical day varies between summer and winter. In summer, Saturdays are taken up with guest changeovers. This involves not just cleaning but mowing lawns and making repairs. The weekdays are more relaxed, apart from sorting laundry and cooking the occasional dinner for guests. In the winter months Jo and John may have the occasional bed and breakfast guests, but mainly use this time to carry out maintenance, decorating and general improvements. As well as tending to the large garden they had to learn swimming pool maintenance, which was a new and unexpected skill for both of them.

They do not employ any staff so changeover days are very busy, hence guests are asked to arrive no earlier than 4pm, although this is the usual check–in time for French holiday homes. Occasionally they ask friends to help out and vice versa.

Jo and John explained that their marketing is done mainly through the Internet via their own website, which was designed by a friend. You can find them at www.les–taloches.com. They are also included on a number of holiday letting sites, at an annual cost of approximately £450 and they also appear in Alastair Sawday's book of prestigious holiday accommodation, entitled '*Somewhere Special to Stay*'. They describe the Internet as having had a massive impact on their business. They also receive clients via recommendations and word of mouth. Bookings have seen a 200% increase since starting almost three years ago.

'It is vital to put a decent amount in your advertising budget and to keep your sites updated' recommends Jo.

To date their guests have been entirely British, although they have recently received enquiries from some Australians and Americans.

They consider their best qualification for setting up a business overseas came from the time when they changed their lives dramatically in 1996 from Jo's work as Freelance Managing Editor and Proof Reader and John's as a Partner in a Procurement company to running a pub. They found this to be a great challenge and made moving abroad seem easier. The couple have always been prepared to embrace change with open arms.

'We received some great advice and support. People helped us install the technical things like computers and occasionally invited us to dinner when we were exhausted. That sort of help is invaluable,' says Jo.

Their three children, ranging in age from 24 to mid–thirties, remained in the UK. They do visit regularly, although they prefer it to be when there are no guests as Jo and John stick rigidly to their rule that guests have exclusive use of the pools.

Jo and John haven't any definitive plans for the future, 'we are just enjoying life here, but it is a large property, and we are turning 60, so I don't think we can plan to stay at Les Taloches indefinitely', explains John.

Asked if they had any regrets, Jo and John said 'absolutely not. We might be richer but would certainly not be happier.'

JO AND JOHN WOULD LIKE TO SHARE THE FOLLOWING

You can contact Jo and John on: mail@les–taloches.com or www.les–taloches.com

Books

Hampshire, D *Living and Working in France*, Survival Books

Sawday, A *Special Places to Stay Series*, Alastair Sawday Publishing: www.specialplacestostay.com

Hunt, D *Starting and Running a B&B in France*, How To Books

Companies

Oui Can Help: www.french–property–news.com/ouicanhelp.htm

Websites

Visit France: www.VisitFrance.co.uk

Holiday Rentals: www.Holiday–Rentals.com

France One Call: www.Franceonecall.com

Jo and John's Tips

Do lots of research.

Make several trips to the country out of season – 'everywhere looks great when the sun is shining'.

Be realistic. Derelict barns and romantic houses in ruins are enchanting, but may take ages to restore.

You don't have to start from scratch. If you need an income quickly, consider buying an existing business.

Take any learning opportunity offered – you never know when it will become useful.

Be realistic about whether you like 'the public'.

Be patient.

MARIA MCMAHON

Key Information

A career as a recruitment consultant

Age: 47

Nationality: British

Status: Engaged

Countries lived in: Germany, England, Hong Kong and United Arab Emirates since 1998

Qualifications: BA Hons Psychology, Diploma in NLP, Diploma in Secretarial and Office Procedures.

Years on the move: 14

After ten years as a temporary secretary in London, Maria McMahon decided it was time for a change and moved to Dubai to work as marketing manager for a training company. After a short stint in the removals business she decided to set up her own company, Elite HR Solutions, in August 2004.

'I had lots of experience in counselling, training and human resources as well as 15 years using administrative and secretarial skills,' says Maria. 'I knew I could combine the skills and do the job. I had also run two small businesses in London previously and knew that working for myself was the only thing I wanted to do.'

Until recently, setting up a company in Dubai was a tricky business and required a local sponsor who would take the lion's share of the profit. In addition, no expatriate could own property and so opportunities for investment were few. Today, much has changed. Even when Maria came to the area in 1998, the Jebel Ali Freezone was home to 1,300 companies. Yet in the last five years Dubai Media City, Dubai Internet City, Dubai Knowledge Village and Dubai Airport Freezone have been established to offer anyone the chance to start a business without a local sponsor. You can now buy property too and with neither tax nor VAT to pay, living in a land of constant sunshine is appealing.

Yet it has not all been rosy for Maria. She lost her job after 9/11 and started a concierge company, helping others to start their own businesses, but this proved not to be commercially viable.

'I had a few years without a regular income, reached rock bottom, had nothing to spare, frozen credit cards, late payments on my car and everything,' Maria remembers. 'Realising that my core business was actually recruitment meant that I dissolved the concierge company and set up in recruitment instead.'

And now things are going from good to better. In fact things are so good that Maria no longer has to rely on networking, cold calling and marketing to bring in business as all her work now comes from referral. This success is due in part to the fact that to start with she worked really hard at networking, which is now paying dividends.

'When I first came to Dubai I used to network all the time, with every group I could get into. This was necessary as I was working as a marketing manager at the time. I have always been a member of the International Business Women's Group, which has been a brilliant networking forum. I've got business, candidates and support from the group since day one! I'm not sure I'm exactly a brilliant networker, but people do seem to come back to me quite often so I must be doing something right.'

Maria used to belong to the British Business Group and the Dubai International Women's Club too and she believes that networking is a fantastic tool that is excellent for business and for fun. However, after nine years she is a bit tired of it finding that it feels a bit too much like work these days. In addition, she is rather too busy to go to as many events as before. Her networking seems to have paid off as she never needs to advertise in the press.

The office of Elite HR Solutions can be found at Dubai Knowledge Village, where Maria has a desk in an open plan office in the Business Centre, which is her official premises. She also lives in a large villa and frequently works from there.

Setting up the business was pretty straightforward. The licence cost AED30,000 and then office space costs the same every year. In addition she had to pay both AED5,000 deposit and non-refundable joining fees. It took about a week but it can take longer if your paperwork and payments take a bit of time to sort out.

'Computer usage makes up about 80% of my work,' she explains. 'I have to post job specifications, screen the 100 CVs I receive every day, source and liaise with candidates and present lists of shortlisted candidates to the clients. Then, of course I have to interview candidates locally and meet with clients in the conference room at the Knowledge Village or in their offices to discuss their requirements.'

Elite HR helps with a range of positions right from secretarial work to regional country directors in hostile regions of the world. The company's strengths lie in the personal and prompt service they can offer and their excellent clients, whom Maria considers to be her 'only real bosses' frequently compliment her on this. As one of hundreds of recruitment companies in the city, it is Maria's standard of service that sets her apart.

'I like being my own boss, I have no–one to answer to in an office each day and it is up to me to call the shots and make a success of it. I want to keep things small, just enough to keep me earning a reasonable living. I don't want huge offices, tons of staff and big overheads. This would only mean I would have to work harder and worry more about paying the bills. All the same I plan to take on an assistant very shortly.'

While Maria tends to work at least the five and a half day week that is standard in the UAE, she relishes her flexibility and ability to plan her own day every day. Business really took off recently and Maria was thrilled to make more than £15,000 in a couple of days when several candidates matched jobs at the same time, though on average she will place a handful of people a month in the 10 to 60 positions she usually has on her books.

'You can get lucky and make a lot of money if you get good clients who give you decent positions to fill. But you can also waste a lot of time on clients who change their mind, company policy, internal structures and so on after you have done tons of work. As few clients will agree to pay a retainer this can be frustrating. A lot of luck is involved.'

Recruitment is a very wide field, but Maria is able to charge 15% of the annual salary for the first placement, 12% for subsequent and will occasionally negotiate a lower fee, so the business can be pretty lucrative. She would recommend anyone younger than her doing some kind of relevant qualification before embarking on such a profession. Despite this, Maria is clearly a natural for the role, and her experience in marketing and running a business have been invaluable coupled with the network of contacts she had established in the four years running up to Elite's opening. She is proud to have achieved so much in so short a time, having arrived unknown seven years ago to being a well–known and respected face around town.

'I think it is vital that you know yourself and know what you are capable of, what you are prepared to risk or sacrifice and what you will do if you fail,' she advises. 'Then, if you feel you can brave the storm, go for it!'

MARIA WOULD LIKE TO SHARE THE FOLLOWING

You can contact Maria on: maria@elitehrsolutions.com

Websites

Dubai Knowledge Village: www.kv.ae

Dubai Media City: www.dubaimediacity.com

Dubai Internet City: www.dubaiinternetcity.com

GoDubai: www.godubai.com

Books

Dew, P Shoult, A *Doing Business with the United Arab Emirates*, Kogan–Page

Books on setting up in business in Dubai, the Freezone and more: www.crossborder.ae

Organisations

International Business Women's Group: www.ibwgdubai.com

British Business Group: www.britbiz–uae.com

Contact Networking Dubai: www.cnetdubai.com

Maria's Tips

Know yourself and your limitations.

Be prepared for hard work, sacrifice and financial worry.

Have a decent savings account or be prepared to be very brave indeed.

KEVIN MORRISSEY

Key Information

A Career in Computer Hardware Rental

Age: 49

Nationality: British

Status: Separated

Countries lived in: UK and UAE

Qualifications: BSc Aeronautical Engineering, DipTECH Loughborough

Years on the move: 22

Kevin was bored and in a rut one winter's day listening to Capital FM when he heard an advert seeking Yellow Pages' sales reps in Dubai. With nothing to lose, he decided to apply.

That was more than 20 years ago, Christmas1983. Within a month he had moved to Dubai with no idea of what he was letting himself in for or even where he was going to spend the night. 22 years later he is still living in the glitziest city of dreams and now he heads up his own company, called Maclease, which specialises in leasing out Macintosh computer hardware.

'At the time it was a choice between another wet and cold winter or six months in the sun,' says Kevin. The decision wasn't hard to make.

Dubai in the eighties was very different from now.

'Like many people in Dubai at that time, you were dropped in at the deep end,' Kevin explains. 'I found I could lead by example.'

After a brief spell selling advertising space for a computer magazine Kevin was invited to help turn what was essentially a 'market stall' type shop in the middle of town into a real computer shop in an area now known as 'Computer Street'. That business grew from one man to five people over the next three years. From there he was asked to manage a computer maintenance business that wanted to start a sales department. This proved very successful and the business developed from two staff to 15 with an increase in turnover of 5000% in just five years.

'But I wanted a new challenge,' explains Kevin. 'IT leasing was a new idea in this region so I stopped being a manager and became an owner. This was my best choice ever.'

Kevin decided to focus on leasing Macintosh hardware and accessories on the basis that the equipment is good value for money and used extensively by people in the advertising and graphics design fields. PC equipment is comparatively cheaper and less of a specialist market.

'Hardly anybody knows how to set up Macintosh hardware,' says Kevin, 'so I can be a big fish in a fairly small pond,' explains Kevin.

And so it was that after five years of building up and managing other people's companies Kevin started to run Maclease full time from 1993 Most of his clients come from the earlier contacts he had made in advertising companies and designers, areas that tend to prefer Macintosh to PC. Kevin rents a warehouse as his business premises to comply with local legal requirements, which state that companies must operate from separate rented accommodation. However, most of the time he works from home in an air–conditioned, carpeted, converted garage with broadband Internet.

'Luckily I have always been good at maths and tinkering with things,' says Kevin, who, despite his Dubai–based IT experience, has no formal qualifications in IT. He describes every day as being different in the world of computer technical support and says his biggest problem is still the operator rather than the machine, blaming 'the nut on the end of the keyboard!'

Kevin's computer expertise seems to market itself. As part of the package he looks after his clients if anything goes wrong.

'Big cloud of smoke or coffee on the keyboard, or you just forgot which button to press? It's all included in the lease. Of course I try to educate the clients that champagne and keyboards do not mix, but that's the advertising business!'

He has now firmly established himself in a niche market.

'Friends and clients always know that I will do something to solve problems,' he continues. 'I always try to see all clients at least once a month.' Perhaps a bit of a natural networker, he is a keen rugby player and Harley Davidson enthusiast, which keeps him in a position to connect with potential clients and is lucky enough to be able to rely on word of mouth to bring in new business. As an external supplier who gets invited to corporate events he knows his efforts are appreciated.

To stay ahead of the game Kevin realises it's important to keep up to date with the latest equipment and not too become too generalised. 'What hardware I will be renting in a year's time I do not know, but whatever it is, I will find out and I will supply it'.

Kevin needs lots of computers in order to run his business, which makes him very asset rich and sometime rather cash poor. He doesn't have a fixed supplier but tends to shop around for the best deals.

'It depends on the exchange rate,' explains Kevin. 'Macs are cheaper in the US but shipping is costly, the UK is better but recently Sterling has been expensive. Apple dealers here finally gave me a new price locally based on the amount I purchase.'

'My income is based on the number of computers I can afford to buy to rent. A typical system rents for about £80 per month and costs about £1800,' He says. Cash flow can be a problem if people don't pay him on time.

What Kevin really likes about his job is that he is the boss. Though not sure where he might have ended up had he stayed in the UK he says: 'I am as much in control of my life as I could be. The grass looks just as green my side of the fence and we don't get all that rain.' He advises anyone looking for a portable career to just 'go for it' and 'take a step back from the rat race and say *is this what I really need?'*

When it came to setting up Kevin's business in Dubai he needed very little to start with: 'Just a couple of thousand pounds for the legal paperwork, another couple to rent a small office and then a computer or two,' he explains. He recommends that in order to avoid requirements for a local sponsor prospective entrepreneurs visit one of the many free zone areas where legal paperwork can be set up as part of their service. The alternative, and more complex, route is to set up with a local sponsor, as Kevin has done, visit your local economic department to obtain all the forms and have explained to you what you can or cannot do. This then allows you to sell directly into the local market rather than via a distributor.

'Work hard, think smart but most of all enjoy whatever you do, expect a few false starts and remember to smile at lady luck,' advises Kevin. 'Many people have helped me in so many ways but the biggest help has come from those grey people who moan that if only they had done x, y and z. I didn't want to be one of them.'

Kevin's next venture is a DVD renting business which should be up and running in 2006, once he has sufficient range and depth of movies available and has his website launched.

'I intend to start so that your first visit leaves the impression that just about every title under the sun is available,' explains Kevin, 'Of course all this is local laws permitting. That means no XXX stuff.'

KEVIN WOULD LIKE TO SHARE THE FOLLOWING

You can contact Kevin on: maclease@emirates.net.ae.

Websites

UAE Yellow Pages: www.dubaiclassified.com
www.uae–ypages.com

UAE Harley Davidson club: www.harley–uae.com

Dubai Rugby clubs: www.dubaiexiles.com
www.rugby7.com

All clubs in UAE: www.emiratesnetwork.com

Dubai Knowledge Village: www.kv.ae

Dubai Media City: www.dubaimediacity.com

Dubai Internet City: www.dubaiinternetcity.com

GoDubai: www.godubai.com

Books

Dew, P, Shoult, A *Doing Business with the United Arab Emirates*, Kogan–Page

Books on setting up in business in Dubai, the Freezone and more: www.crossborder.ae

Organisations

British Business Group: www.britbiz–uae.com

Kevin's Tips

Find something you like doing and that will pay the bills.

Stay on top of the game, keep your knowledge/skills up to date.

It's never too late to start (again).

JANE COLMAN

Key Information

A career in teaching and love of the arts

Age: 53

Nationality: British

Status: Divorced with two children

Countries lived in: England and Qatar

Qualifications: BA in English and Drama and a BEd.

Years on the move: 28

Charlie and Jane had met whilst first year students in London and married in 1974, shortly after graduating. Both had started work straight away: Jane as an English and Drama teacher in a multi–racial comprehensive school in East Acton, Charlie as a mechanical engineer with a large firm in Ealing.

'Charlie was passionate about his work and we hardly saw each other during the weekdays. Our marriage was in trouble, but as working individuals we were successful; both climbing the career ladder rapidly and gaining responsibility and promotion,' she says.

When Charlie was asked by his firm to go to Qatar in the spring of 1977, they both jumped at the chance. Charlie would be the second–in–command of a newly opened office with a variety of projects in an oil–rich, developing country. There was a large expatriate community already established and, filled with the optimism of youth, Jane had assumed that there would be plenty of opportunities for her to work too. With a combined degree in English and Drama plus a qualification in teaching, Jane felt ready to face the challenge. However, things were not as wonderful as she first expected.

'I became my husband's appendage,' she remembers. Many expatriate accompanying partners may empathise with this feeling.

Jane had only just learned to drive before going to Qatar. She realised that living in such heat would mean that driving would be a must. Expats tended to live in clusters on the outside of the city of Doha, in the middle of a desert wasteland, and there was nothing but sand, tarmac and building sites for miles.

'I had two months to learn to drive,' says Jane. 'You could say it was a crash course – and I failed my test anyway.'

In Qatar, there was a six–day working week – like all Muslim countries, Friday was the weekend – and the working day started early, whilst still comparatively cool, with a three–hour lunch break and finished at about 6.30pm. So Jane found herself unable to drive and stranded at home.

'I soon realised that I was going to have to work, just to get out of the house. I was looking at walls, had no conversation with anyone and I felt isolated. Charlie was far busier than he had been back home in the UK, but this time, I didn't have any friends or a life of my own and the chances of meeting anybody were slim,' she says.

On consideration, Jane thought that her best option would be to employ her skills as a teacher. Not only was she trained in this area but she looked upon it as her vocation. She had, however done little research before leaving the UK and in those days, virtually nobody had heard of the Internet. With few contacts in Qatar and no driving licence, Jane was somewhat restricted and found herself becoming increasingly dispirited. Finally, an associate of her husband pointed out that although there were no secondary level English speaking schools in the area, there was a primary school and a branch of the British Council, the UK's international organisation for educational opportunities and cultural relations. Despite the fact that Jane had no formal TEFL (Teaching English as a Foreign Language) qualification, she felt confident that she would be able to teach her native language all the same. Indeed, Jane managed to find a couple of evening classes to teach and the hourly pay was surprisingly high.

'I could only teach groups of women,' she explains; 'men had to have a male teacher, but this was better than nothing and I enjoyed the challenge of learning how to teach English as a foreign language. The women were delightful and their English was really very good anyway. They also needed to get out of the house, I think, most of them were Lebanese and therefore, Westernised in their dress and attitudes, so we learned a lot from each other.'

'I gained two private pupils too – sisters, Fatma and Miriam, who were married to Qatari Sheikhs and were very young mothers. They would send a chauffeur–driven limo to take me to their palatial villas and we would talk about my way of life in England. They had both travelled around the world but had never mixed with the natives!'

In the meantime, Jane was gradually meeting more expats through Charlie's work contacts. She soon discovered that a new English theatre had been finished just before her arrival and since, as she explains, television consisted only of Arab programmes, old episodes of 'Kojak' and the English news at 6.00pm, any English entertainment was always a sell–out. Jane auditioned for that good old English institution, pantomime, in the autumn and landed the role of Dick Whittington.

'There is something even more bizarre than normal about a woman, playing a boy and slapping her fish–netted thigh in Arabian climes, but I met lots of fellow thespians and made good friends and more importantly I felt fulfilled doing something I enjoyed,' she recalls.

Through networking amongst a relatively small group, Jane's opportunities for work snowballed and she found that there were in fact numerous ways in which she could make use of what she considered her key skills.

One thing led to another and she made friends with a guy called Trevor, who worked as an architect but also presented a sports programme and a music request show on the radio. The English–speaking radio station was hugely popular and provided a much needed communication lifeline for the expat community. So when Trevor offered to introduce her to a producer of radio plays, Jane jumped at the chance seizing another opportunity that was afforded her.

'This was one opportunity, I definitely would not have had at home!' she says. 'I even found myself being interviewed for their 'Desert Island Discs' programme, as a celebrity of stage and radio, the following summer!'

Jane did however experience setbacks; such as when the British Council had to cut back on part–time staff and Jane's position was one of the first to go at the end of her first year in Qatar. However with her ever–increasing list of contacts and skills it wasn't long before she found a new position, this time as an assistant in a hotel's newspaper and bookshop. Again, this opportunity came about through her connections.

'This was a fascinating mixture of work,' says Jane. Not only did her new role consist of stocking the shelves with all the latest paperbacks for hotel guests and expats, but she was also responsible for reviewing all the new titles and authors; the perfect role for an English graduate with a passion for literature.

By now Jane had passed her driving test and really enjoyed the part of her new job, which meant she had to drive to the airport every morning to clear newspapers and magazines through customs and the censors' office.

'My job was to bring the European papers and periodicals back to the shop, suitably cut and blacked out, yet I had been privy to the censored news!' she remembers.

Jane stayed in this job for her remaining year in Qatar and returned to England when Charlie's contract expired. Jane has now returned to her original vocation, teaching and has built a new life with Trevor.

'I am passionate about my job, a born teacher. I have always enjoyed seeing young people fulfilling a creative side through writing creatively and using drama as a means of expression, gaining confidence and learning. It gives me enormous pleasure to create value and reveal potential in the individual. Teaching is a means of providing a sense of hope for the future, for every young person,' she says.

Jane is a firm believer in grasping whatever opportunities life presents you with and thinks that going to Qatar all those years ago was the start of many a new 'Road Less Travelled'.

'I wouldn't have missed taking them for the world,' she says.

JANE WOULD LIKE TO SHARE THE FOLLOWING

You can contact Jane on: JaneColman@aol.com

For further information on opportunities offered by the British Council, please go to: www.britishcouncil.org

Advertised English Language jobs worldwide at: www.elgazette.com

Bridge Linguatec Language Services: www.bridgelinguatec.com

Dave's ESL Café: www.eslcafe.com

Teacher Training Agency: www.tda.gov.uk/Recruit.aspx

Times Education Supplement: www.tes.co.uk

Times Educational Supplement Jobs: www.tesjobs.co.uk

Consultants in Independent School Education: www.gabbitas.co.uk

Council of International Schools: www.cois.org

World–wide Education Service: www.wesworldwide.com

The International Schools Service: www.iss.edu

Books

Swan, M *Practical English Usage*, Oxford University Press

Harmer, J *The Practice of English Language Teaching (LHLT)*, Longman

McKay, S.L *Teaching English Overseas: An Introduction*, Oxford University Press

Target, F *Working in English Language Teaching*, Kogan Page

Teach Abroad: The Complete International Guide to Teaching Opportunities Overseas, The Central Bureau

Marguerite, E *Teaching Abroad*, The Institute of International Education

Jane's Tips

Be flexible: be prepared think laterally and diversify.

Run a club: if you can run a hobby group in an area that interests you and is allied to your business, you will make friends and ultimately new clients too.

Do work that is associated with the things you love: and you will stay motivated and interested.

FRANCES RYAN

Key information

Psychomotor Therapist, Remedial Educator, Photographer and Adventurer

Age: 60

Nationality: British

Status: Single

Countries lived in: England, Australia, India, France, Malta

Qualifications: State Diploma in Psychomotor Therapy and Remedial Education, Sorbonne Faculty of Medicine; Internships in the UK. Sunshine Homes for the Blind, Cologne Centre for Motor Re–education. Quebec University course for Instrumental Enrichment Program (Feuerstein).

Years on the move: 34

Very few people can claim to have had a life quite as interesting as Frances. Amongst the more memorable points are working with the flying doctors in Australia, helping with aboriginal relocation and assisting Mother Teresa. Her wanderlust began when she was just 14 and read Marco Polo.

Frances has spent much of her life working with special needs children, a role that she describes as: 'Demanding, exacting, amazing and rewarding.'

The route that brought Frances to her work as a psychomotor therapist has been circuitous. Having failed her A levels, she spent a brief stint appeasing her parents at secretarial college before moving onto bigger and better things. At this time Frances had no firm career plans, instead she envisaged a career as a 'marine biologist, journalist or maybe an explorer.'

Bored with Britain she set off to visit her grandfather in Australia. Although a descendant of a Balkanese Count he had emigrated there years earlier, leaving much of his family behind in the UK.

'The Balkanese have a saying that those with wanderlust live under a 'bleeding star', so I guess that's me,' she says.

After working in Sydney learning the hotel business Frances decided she needed a road trip. So she bought a second hand VW Beetle, put a tent in the back, stocked up with cartons of baby–food as rations and set off. She drove a total of 25,000 miles, working as a 'Jillaroo'– a rancher/farmhand – in New South Wales before setting off to the Great Barrier Reef where she worked as a crew member on 'The New Endeavour'– a three–masted schooner sailing the islands with tourist passengers.

After surviving shipwreck, when the First Mate got drunk on a very stormy night, she was soon on the move again, driving through Mount Isa to Alice Springs, which at that time consisted of a gum tree, a couple of dozen houses and the spring. Here she met an American who was compiling the first aboriginal dictionary. Intrigued, Frances started spending time on the Aborigine reserve working with the local personnel.

'It was very difficult to communicate with the Aborigines; I felt very sorry for them to be displaced in the way that they had, but being young and inexperienced I followed instructions and did as I was told,' she says.

During this time, Frances also found herself working with the flying doctors, and, although she had no formal medical training, her practicality and adaptable nature proved invaluable.

You might have thought that after her escapades in Australia, Frances would have been keen to return to a quieter existence. But no sooner had she arrived back in the UK than Frances joined up with the sister ship of the New Endeavour to sail from Ramsgate to Australia. By this point Frances's parents had not seen her for almost three years and it seemed that their daughter attracted action wherever she went. During the following few years she was part of the Hong Kong riots, the six day Egyptian war and the Greek coup d'état ...

This proved too much for her mother who then went to desperate lengths to try and encourage her daughter to stay safe and closer to home. Indeed, she did apply for jobs while her mother tempted her with breakfast in bed. Before long Frances was helping Wally Herbert organise his dream of crossing the Arctic Ocean with dogs and sledges. After a hectic nine months of organisation she finally arrived at base camp in the Arctic Circle. Here she worked for three weeks, the only woman among 250 men, sorting out parachute supply drops.

City life was never to be and when a friend mentioned that she wanted to go to India, Frances was determined to go along and began planning how to avoid the monsoons and keep her next adventure secret from her mother right away.

The planning took more than a year and so it was that in 1969 Frances spent nine months away, covering 25,000 miles travelling around India and back to Europe. By this point Frances was so impoverished that she slept in her car in the Avenue George V!

Her love of adventure was here to stay but Frances was sensible enough to realise that she needed to fund the trips she adored. She had always wanted to live in Paris and decided it was the perfect base from which she could earn the money to finance her adventures. Initially it was her hotel experience and secretarial training that enabled her to get a job as a PA to an American entrepreneur. It wasn't long before she could return to India and in 1971 enjoyed a hard trip overland. The trip led her to realise that she really wanted to do something 'worthy' and so began the next chapter of her life.

An Anglo–Indian nun friend introduced Frances to Mother Teresa in Calcutta and it was not long before she was helping local destitute adolescents find work and develop a sense of self.

'This was one of the happiest moments of my life,' she recalls. 'In fact it was Mother Teresa herself who encouraged me to obtain qualifications that were applicable to caring for others.'

So Frances returned to Paris, this time to study psychomotor therapy. The psychomotor diploma is a three year paramedical degree allowing her to work with children in any area in which they may need help. Over time, she has come to specialise in pre–teenagers with both physical and emotional issues, though the approach itself is physiological with a psychological goal, based on games and movement,

'If you want to do this kind of work I don't believe that there is a specific qualification or route into this field. It is more important that you have experience of life and of dealing with people that you can draw on personal experience and empathise with individuals is vital. An ability to remain a dispassionate observer, to observe without judging and not be afraid of acting spontaneously with both children and parents are all–important,' she explains.

Frances feels that psychomotor therapy is the perfect portable career as all schools are in need of special educators, although some are still unwilling to admit this. If you combine your professional qualifications with a love of sport and human nature then you can adapt to anywhere. This approach has put her at the forefront of psychomotor and special education on an international level.

Since becoming a therapist, Paris has largely remained Frances's home although she was temporarily based in Malta. While there Frances directed the re–organisation of facilities serving severely handicapped children where she liaised between the Maltese government, UNESCO and families. The parents' support group, which she founded there is celebrating its 30th anniversary this year and is considered a model for Europe.

In Paris, Frances introduced psychomotor therapy to the English–speaking community and in 1986, having realised how few facilities there were for special needs Anglophone children in Paris Ideas and New Techniques (SPRINT) and Sprint's Parent Action Network (SPAN) were born. SPRINT is specifically a European network for special educators offering resources to the Anglophone community. SPAN is SPRINT's parental support group for the parents of such children. Since their formation, SPRINT and SPAN have become worldwide networks for until 1997. More recently SPRINT has created Special Training and Education Programme (STEP) to allow members of SPRINT and SPAN to provide diverse training and educational programmes for parents and professionals.

Frances has maintained private practices in Paris and Monaco, lectures extensively on early childhood, learning disabilities and the link between motor and cognitive functioning, and frequently works as a mediator between children, teachers, parents, schools and governments.

'I tend to earn between £40 and £80 an hour,' she says. 'Though I grab any opportunity I can to speak at educational conferences and at international schools too, which can earn me around £700 a day.'

Frances has always been one to grab any opportunity that comes her way and the work in Monaco came about as a result of a recommendation, which first saw her in the principality delivering a workshop.

'In the end I was going there every month for about five days,' she remembers.

About 15 years ago, Frances began diving and discovered an underwater world that she finds as fascinating as land travel and in 1997 she decided to take a year's sabbatical.

'I lived the dream of a lifetime,' she recalls. 'With a back pack on one shoulder and tent and diving equipment on the other, I set off with a diving buddy to dive around the world. We dived 42 islands in the South Pacific, getting in just ahead of El Nino.'

Ever–resourceful and unafraid of hard work Frances did all she could to fund the trip, selling her car, renting out her apartment and holding down two jobs. So, in addition to her therapy work she helped to organise a world veterinary congress, entailing 10 hours a day in front of a computer screen – her worst nightmare.

And it was during her sabbatical that she developed a love of black and white photography and thus added another income stream to her portfolio of careers. Since 1999 Frances has participated in a number of exhibitions and sold many of her works. She sells a 30 x 40 cm print for €200 typically.

The three very full days she spends working in her 'day–job' can be so intense that Frances recognises the need to relax and switch off. This is one of the reasons that she enjoys photography so much and devotes the rest of her time to that.

'I find it therapeutic,' she says. 'You are forced to focus completely on the task in hand and block out any other intrusions, especially in the dark room.'

Her black and white compositions isolate the effects of light and shadow on substance and become in themselves a form of meditation for the viewer.

Frances underlines the importance of taking time out to rebalance both body and mind. She practises Chinese Qi Gong, similar to Tai Chi, each morning to give her greater awareness of the harmony between mind and body. She firmly believes that it has benefited her body as she has not taken traditional medicine for over ten years.

Indeed, one of the first qualities that anyone notices about Frances is her great personal warmth. This characteristic, which has grown over the years, allows her to be an effective mediator. Frances admits that mothers, whatever their culture, like to talk to her as a woman and respond positively to her empathy.

She may be 60 now but Frances is not ready to relax just yet.

'I can't afford to retire yet, because in France you do not get a full pension unless you have worked for a full 37 years here. So I plan to have some more adventures by renting out my apartment,' she says, happy to be a 'bouncing 60', which entitles her to cheap travel.

FRANCES WOULD LIKE TO SHARE THE FOLLOWING

You can contact Frances on: fryan@club–internet.fr

Organisations

Europe's Children Our Concern – Supporting children and young people with learning difficulties [Previously known as European Children in Crisis (ECIC)]: www.ecoc.be

SPRINT
(Sharing Professional Resources Ideas and New Techniques)
Michelle Bennani–Smires
Secretary/SPRINT
51, rue de Navarre
78490 Montfort l'Amaury
FRANCE
01 34 86 93 41
sprint.france@free.fr
http://sprint.france.free.fr/sprint.html

SPAN (Sprint Parents' Action Network)
Secretary: Leslie Palanker
34 rue Bassano, 75008 Paris
Telephone: 02 33 21 48 16
SPAN@freesurf.fr

Frances' Tips

Have a direction rather than a fixed goal allowing one's mind to be more open when offered opportunities.

Seize linked opportunities looking upon them as stepping stones or means to an end rather than ends in themselves

Learn how to say 'I don't know but could find out!'

Understand that quite often aggression from the other person is due to the fact that they are not feeling so good about themselves – unless of course you aggressed first!

Believe in yourself.

Be disciplined, respectful and polite.

Have a sense of humour, especially being able to laugh at yourself and accept that you will make mistakes.

Where In The World

Here is a selection of the most useful websites that will get you started on the research you need to make your dream of living and working abroad into a reality.

ANDORRA

The Andorran Embassy: www.andorra.be/en/2.4.htm

Chamber of Commerce Andorra: www.ccis.ad

Summary of Business Laws in Andorra:
www.lowtax.net/lowtax/html/janolaw.html

Open a bank account in Andorra: www.creditandorra.ad

Andorra Business Directory: www.can–wtd.com/dir/ANDORRA

Useful Websites

List of Andorran embassies worldwide:
http://www.embassiesabroad.com/embassies–of/Andorra.cfm#3681

General information on Andorra:
http://www.tiscali.co.uk/reference/encyclopaedia/countryfacts/andorra.html

Tip

Make sure you stay on the right side of the law by checking out this directory of English speaking lawyers in Andorra:

www.hierosgamos.org/hg/db_lawfirms.asp?action=search&subcategory=Business%7CLaw&country=Andorra

AUSTRALIA

Australian Embassy:www.australia.org.uk

Chamber of Commerce: www.acci.asn.au

Tax office: www.ato.gov.au

Where to go for advice on setting up a business:
www.business.gov.au

Directory of banks: www.qualisteam.com/Banks/Pacific/Australia

Useful Websites

Australian Visa Bureau: www.visabureau.co.uk/australia

Australian Migration Experts: www.migrationbureau.com

Further information on taxation:
www.australian–embassy.nl/content.cfm?pagina=327

Tip

Remember to get you company's name registered. Check out this site for further information:

www.incorporator.com.au/business_registration_register_business_name_search.asp

AUSTRIA

Austrian Embassy

http://www.austria.org.uk

Chamber of Commerce: http://portal.wko.at

Tax office:
www.help.gv.at/Content.Node/144/Seite.1440000.html#Tax

Where to go for advice on setting up a business:
www.help.gv.at/Content.Node/144/Seite.1440000.html

Somewhere to open a bank account in English translation:
www.oenb.at/en/ueber_die_oenb
rechtl_grundlagen/rechtliche_grundlagen.jsp

Useful Websites

American Chamber of Commerce in Austria: www.amcham.or.at

Austrian Association of Commercial Agents:
www.commercial–agent.at

Austrian Business Circle: www.austrianbc.co.za

Tip

Check out this great website for information on Austrian Business etiquette to give you that competitive edge.

http://www.executiveplanet.com/business–etiquette/Austria.html

BELGIUM

Belgian Embassy: www.diplobel.org/uk

Chamber of Commerce: www.cci.be

Directory of banks: www.bnb.be

Tax office: www.taxsites.com/international/belgium.html

Where to go for advice on setting up a business: http://invest.belgium.be/settingup/?a=5441

Useful Websites

Tips on choosing a bank in Belgium: www.expatica.com/source/site_article.asp?subchannel_id=43&story_id=1468&name=Tips+for+choosing+a+bank

Reports on Belgium business customs, practices, etiquette, negotiating and Belgian business protocol, cross–cultural communication: www.worldbiz.com/bizbelgium.html

Belgium's business news magazine: www.brusselsreview.com

Belgian business directory: www.businesspatrol.com/businesspatrol_links.php3?topic=Belgium

Tip

Network with other business and potential clients. Check out the Association of Belgian Business Clubs for further details – www.diplomatie.be/en/addresses/abroad/bbclubs.asp

BULGARIA

Bulgarian Embassy: www.bulgarianembassy.org.uk

Chamber of Commerce: www.bcci.bg

Tax office: www.taxadmin.minfin.bg/eng/great_britain.pdf

Useful websites

Bulgarian leader's forum: www.bblf.bg/news.php?cat_id=1

Bulgarian Business Advisor: www.bba.bg

Information on buying property in Bulgaria: www.bestbulgarianrealestate.com/menu/legal–advice

The Bulgarian stock exchange: www.bse–sofia.bg

General information on the media in Bulgaria: www.bulgaria.com

Tip

Keep abreast of business developments and opportunities in Bulgaria. Check out the business daily online pages at: www.pari.bg

CANADA

Canadian Embassy: www.canada.org.uk

Chamber of Commerce: www.chamber.ca

Tax office: www.cra–arc.gc.ca/contact/tso–e.html

Advice on setting up a business: www.sbinfocanada.about.com

Canadian National Bank: www.cibc.com

Useful websites

General business information: www.canadianbusiness.com

General list of banks in Canada:
www.businessjeeves.ca/Banks.html

More advice on starting a business:
www.canadaone.com/tools/startingabusiness.html

Advice on loans for small business:
www.wd.gc.ca/finance/programs/microABLED_e.asp

Tip

For networking in Canada with Canada's greatest networker, Donna Messer, go to www.connectuscanada.com

CHINA

Chinese Embassy: www.chinese–embassy.org.uk

Chamber of commerce: www.cgcc.org.hk

Tax office:
www.pwchk.com/home/eng/prctax_corp_repre_office.htm

Advice on setting up a business:
www.buyusa.gov/china/en/doingbizinchina.html

Useful Websites

Guide to doing business in China:
www.executiveplanet.com/business–etiquette/China.html

China Council for the Promotion of International Trade:
www.ccpit.org

Details of Chinese business ventures:
www.chinavista.com/business/home.html

Business China information centre: www.export.gov/china

Tip

Check out this great site for up to date information on China. The largest English portal in China, providing news, business info, and learning materials: www.chinadaily.com

CROATIA

Croatian Embassy: croatia.embassyhomepage.com

Chamber of Commerce: www.hgk.hr

Tax office: www.internationalbudget.org/cdrom/papers/tax/croatiatax.htm

Advice on setting up a business: www.delalb.cec.eu.int/al/eu_in_see/regional_cro.htm

Croatian Banks: www.portalino.it/banks/_hr.htm

Useful websites

Croatian business news: www.croatianmall.com/links.htm

Croatian Business Directories: www.4icj.com/hr/04–business–directories–companies.htm

List of Croatian Business services available online: www.croatiasa.com/category/1/

Tip

Don't forget – network, network, network! Checkout this website for more details www.croatian.net

CYPRUS

Cypriot Embassy: www.cyprus.embassyhomepage.com

Chamber of Commerce:
www.esc.eu.int/president/speeches/docs/Briesch_nicosie_100204_en.pdf

Tax office: www.lowtax.net/lowtax/html/jcydctx.html

Advice on setting up a business:
www.britishhighcommission.gov.uk/.../Xcelerate/ShowPage&c=Page&cid=1042219962607

Cypriot Banks:
www.worldwide–tax.com/cyprus/cypinvestbanks.asp

Useful websites

Business directory: www.cyprusyellowpages.com

The inside line on corporate etiquette in Cyprus:
www.worldbiz.com/index.php/cPath/44

Tip

Get to know how your new country works inside out. Have a look at www.lowtax.net/lowtax/html/jcycfir.html for more information on business infrastructure in Cyprus

CZECH REPUBLIC

Czech Embassy: www.mzv.cz/london

Chamber of Commerce: www.britcham.cz

Tax office:
www.mfcr.cz/cps/rde/xchg/ mfcr/hs.xsl/en_tax_affairs.html

Confederation of Industry of the Czech Republic:
http://prague.tv/prague/finance/chambers–of–commerce/3452

Czech banks: www.prague–czech.cz/htm/business/banks.php

Useful websites

Czech business weekly, Online weekly newspaper, Information from the Czech Republic: www.cbw.cz/phprs

The official site for business professionals searching for information, assistance, or contacts on business activities in the Czech Republic: www.businessinfo.cz/en

Czech business directory: www.czechinfocenter.com/dir

Tip

Lifestyle is also key to enjoying your new country, Check out www.prague–tribune.cz for both business and lifestyle information.

DENMARK

Danish Embassy: www.denmark.org.uk

Chamber of Commerce: www.ipc.um.dk/en/servicemenu/Links/PublicAdministration/TheDanishChamberOfCommerce/

Advice on setting up a business: www.worldbiz.com/denmark.html

Tax office: www.tax.dk/english.htm

Danish banks: www.ezilon.com/regional/denmark/business_and_economy/banking_and_finance/index.shtml

Useful websites

Further Danish Tax information: www.taxsites.com/international/denmark.html

Information on getting a Danish bank account: www.ruc.dk/humbas_en/FAQ_Int/Bank_account

Advice on the financial implications of relocating: www.alldenmark.dk/package.htm

Tip

It pays to know the business history of the country you are going to live in, Here is an excellent website to get to know the business history of Denmark in the last 200 years: www.sa.dk/ea/aabtid/engdefault.htm

FRANCE

French Embassy: www.ambafrance–uk.org

Chamber of Commerce: www.ccfgb.co.uk/en/home/home.asp

Tax office: www.intransit–international.com/life_paris_tax.html

Advice on setting up a business:
www.executiveplanet.com/business–etiquette/France.html

French Banks: www.portalino.it/banks/_fr.htm

Useful websites

Guide to French business: www.actufax.com

Practices and protocol in French business:
www.worldbiz.com/bizfrance.html

Tip

Acquiring business language is key to succeeding in your chosen country, Here's a great website to help you get you head around business French:

http://french.about.com/library/weekly/aa111000.htm

FINLAND

Finland Embassy: www.finemb.org.uk

Chamber of Commerce: www.turku.chamber.fi/english/index.php

Tax office:
www.vero.fi/default.asp?language=ENG&domain=VERO_ENGLISH

Advice on setting up a business:
http://www.suomi.fi/english/employment_and_entrepreneurship/entrepreneurship

Finnish Banks: www.portalino.it/banks/_fi.htm

Useful websites

Reports on doing business in Finland, business customs and protocol: www.worldbiz.com/finland.html

A selection of business web sites in Finland:
www.businesspatrol.com/businesspatrol_links.php3?topic=Finland

Summary of Country Services for Finland Page from *The Internationalist*: www.internationalist.com/business/Finland.php

Expatriate resources:
www.escapeartist.com/embassy29/finland2.html

Tip

To really understand about the Finns read *'Finland – Cultural Lone Wolf'* by Richard Lewis and available from Nicholas Brealey www.nbrealey–books.com

GERMANY

German Embassy: www.german–embassy.org.uk

Chamber of Commerce: www.germanbritishchamber.co.uk

Tax office: www.destatis.de/e_home.htm

Advice on setting up a business: www.germany–info.org/relaunch/business/doing_business/settingup.html

German banks: www.germanbanks.org

Useful websites

Information on German business law: www.germanbusinesslaw.de

German Business association: www.germancentre.com

Sample German business letters: www.german.about.com/library/blbiz_brief01.htm

Altavista's Translation Site Links for Business German: www.isu.edu/~nickcrai/gepublic.html

Tip

Learn to do business the German way. Find out about the ins and outs of German business practice at: www.german–way.com/biz.html

GREECE

Greek Embassy: www.greekembassy.org.uk

Chamber of Commerce: www.acci.gr/en_index2.htm

Tax office: www.taxsites.com/international/greece.html

Advice on setting up a business:
www.helleniccomserve.com/settingupbusinessgreece.html

Greek banks: www.hellascapital.ca/greekbanks.htm

Useful websites

Greek business directory: www.hellasob.com/direct

Further business listings: www.evresi.gr/data/index.php

Greek business forum: www.greekbiz.com/index.jsp?context=101

Tip

Get up to date with native business thought. Check out these articles written by Greek business professionals: www.hellasob.com/bt

HONG KONG

Chinese Embassy: china.embassyhomepage.com

Chamber of Commerce: www.chamber.org.hk/business_world_h.asp

Tax office: www.taxsites.com/international/hongkong.html

Advice on setting up a business: www.investhk.gov.hk/category.aspx?lang=1&code=IHK2–SETTINGHK

Hong Kong banks: www.hkab.org.hk

Useful websites

Business development website: www.business.gov.hk/bep/opencms/release/eng

Trade Development Council portal with business database and resources for businesses in Hong Kong: www.tdctrade.com

Hong Kong business directory: www.chamber.org.hk/hkdir

Tip

See both sides of the financial and social scene with information form at: www.thestandard.com.hk

HUNGARY

Hungarian Embassy: www.huemblon.org.uk

Chamber of Commerce: www.unioncamere.net/cei/hungary.htm

Tax office: http://www.meh.hu/english

Where to go for advice on setting up a business: www.itdh.hu/itdh/nid/Regulations

Somewhere to open a bank account in English translation: www.offshoreinfo.com/ord/hubkord.htm

Useful websites

Further advice on setting up a bank account: youth.cec.eu.int/movingeu/en/host/EN.Hungary.htm

The Budapest business journal: www.bbj.hu

Tip

See this handy website for converting and recognizing Hungarian currency: www.budapesthotels.com/touristguide/Money.asp

INDIA

Indian Embassy: www.hcilondon.org

Chamber of Commerce: www.indianchamber.org

Tax office: incometaxindia.gov.in

Where to go for advice on setting up a business: www.indax.com/business.html

Open a bank account: www.icicibank.com/pfsuser/icicibank/ibank–nri/nrinewversion/faq_nri.htm

Useful websites

Indian business directory: www.indianyellowpages.com

Business information: www.tribuneindia.com/2005/20050105/biz.htm

Examination of business and tax issues in India: http://www.outsource2india.com/services/tax.asp

Tip

Here is the very useable website of India's national daily newspaper, a handy resource: www.timesofindia.indiatimes.com

ITALY

Italian Embassy: www.embitaly.org.uk

Chamber of Commerce: www.italchambers.net

Tax office: www.vasapolli.it/doing_bussines.htm

Where to go for advice on setting up a business: www.expatsinitaly.com

Open a bank account: www.poste.it/en/bancoposta/conti/business_account.shtml

Useful websites

Italian business etiquette: www.executiveplanet.com/business-etiquette/Italy.html

Italian business service: www.stelnet.com

Tip

For information on setting up a business in Italy written by both a Brit and an Italian go to www.howtoitaly.com

JAPAN

Japanese Embassy: www.uk.emb–japan.go.jp/

Chamber of Commerce: www.jcciny.org

Tax office: www.vasapolli.it/doing_bussines.htm

Where to go for advice on setting up a business:
www.simul.co.jp/en/about/casestudy.html

Open a bank account:
www.japan.com/living/money/banks/account.php

English language website for the Bank of Japan: www.boj.or.jp/en

Useful websites

Tokyo Chamber of Commerce: www.tokyo–cci.or.jp/english

Essential information for living in Japan:
www.jetsetjapan.com/infozone–money–bank.shtml

Tip

For girls going to Japan to live and work see the work of Caroline Pover who wrote 'Being a Broad in Japan', at: www.being–a–broad.com

LUXEMBOURG

Luxembourg Embassy: www.luxembourg–usa.org

Chamber of Commerce: www.cc.lu

Tax office: www.taxsites.com/international/luxembourg.html

Where to go for advice on setting up a business:
http://www.pwcglobal.com/lu/eng/ins–sol/publ/pwc_luxloc.pdf

Open a bank account: www.fortisbanque.lu/bank/index–en.html

Useful websites

A useful business directory:
www.bizeurope.com/bsr/country/luxem.htm

A great guide to doing business:
www.internationalist.com/business/Luxembourg.php

Keep an eye on business developments in Luxembourg:
www.einnews.com/luxembourg/newsfeed–LuxembourgBusiness

Tip

An English–speaking forum for contact and communication among decision makers, opinion formers and participants in Luxembourg's local and international can be found at: www.bcc.lu

MOROCCO

Morocco Embassy: www.morocco.embassyhomepage.com

Chamber of Commerce: www.amcham–morocco.com

Tax office: casablanca.usconsulate.gov/irs / income_tax2.html

Where to go for advice on setting up a business: www.allbusiness.com/periodicals/topic/2384399–1–2.html

Open a bank account: http://www.bkam.ma

Useful websites

More information about the country: www.arab.net/morocco

Get a sense of the cultural scene. Check out this excellent website: www.africa.upenn.edu/Country_Specific/Morocco.html

Daily news on the Moroccan next work: www.moroccodaily.com

Tip

To get to know the country inside out, check out this website: www.odci.gov/cia/publications/factbook/print/mo.html

THE NETHERLANDS

Dutch Embassy: www.netherlands–embassy.org.uk

Chamber of Commerce or equivalent: www.kamervankoophandel.nl

Tax office: www.belastingdienst.nl

Somewhere to open a bank account with English translation: www.abn–amro.nl

Useful websites

Site with jobs, housing, regulations and much more that focuses on Netherlands, Germany, France, Belgium and Spain: www.expatica.com

Site for voluntary organisation offering advice, telephone helpline, counselling and factsheets for newcomers: www.access–nl.org

Information on Amsterdam: www.amsterdam.com

Information on The Hague: www.denhaag.com

Lots about The Hague including translations of some documents: www.thehagueonline.com

Tip

Books on every aspect of life in Holland available from www.hollandbooks.nl and the annual Holland Handbook contains everything you could ever want to know about living and working here.

NEW ZEALAND

New Zealand Embassy: www.nzembassy.com/home.cfm?c=31

Chamber of Commerce: www.nzchambers.co.nz

Tax office: www.treasury.govt.nz/tax

Where to go for advice on setting up a business: www.nzte.govt.nz/section/11735.aspx

Open a bank account: www.nationalbank.co.nz

Useful websites

New Zealand business round up: www.nbr.co.nz

New Zealand business yellow pages: www.yellowpages.co.nz

The latest business news, opinion and financial markets reports from New Zealand: www.nzherald.co.nz/section/index.cfm?c_id=3

The New Zealand business round table: www.nzbr.org.nz

Tip

Direct access to the official government register and national database which stores registration information – companies, trademarks, industrial information: www.companies.govt.nz/pls/web/dbssiten.main

NORWAY

Norway Embassy: www.norway.org.uk

Chamber of Commerce: www.chamber.no

Tax office: www.norway.org.uk/policy/tax

Where to go for advice on setting up a business: www.norway.com/businesslinks

Open a bank account: www.norwaysavingsbank.com/bankingAgreement.html

Useful website

Advice on doing successful business in Norway: www.businessculture.com/norway

The Oslo Embassy point of contact for business information about Norway: www.usa.no/norway/business.html

Advice on successfully doing business in Norway: www.norway.com/businesslinks

Tip

Find out more about living in Norway from the experts who wrote 'Living in Norway' and available from the American Women's Club of Oslo at www.awcoslo.org

PORTUGAL

Portuguese Embassy: www.portugal.embassyhomepage.com

Chamber of Commerce: www.port–chambers.com

Tax office: www.fco.gov.uk/Files/kfile/taking_residence,0.pdf

Where to go for advice on setting up a business: www.shelteroffshore.com/index.php/living/more/working_in_portugal

Open a bank account:
www.worldwide–tax.com/portugal/porinvestbanks.asp

Useful Websites

The Lisbon Trade Association:
www.port–chambers.com/eng/arbit_arbit.htm

Bank of Portugal: www.bportugal.pt

Business Directory: www.portugaloffer.com

Tip

Official site of the government agency Investments, Trade and Tourism of Portugal at: www.portugal.org

RUSSIA

Russian Embassy: www.rusemblon.org

Chamber of Commerce: http://eng.tpprf.ru/

Tax office: www.waytorussia.net/business/tax.html

Where to go for advice on setting up a business: www.dobusinessinrussia.com/services.html

Open a bank account: www.portalino.it/banks/_ru.htm

Useful websites

Further advice on tax in Russia: www.russianembassy.org/RUSSIA/civil_code.htm

Business information and services for companies wishing to venture into Russia: www.ruscontact.com

News and analysis: http://english.pravda.ru/

Tip

For in depth coverage of Russian politics and business go to: www.bubl.ac.uk/link/r/russianbusiness.htm

SOUTH AFRICA

South African Embassy: www.southafricahouse.com

Chamber of Commerce: www.sacob.co.za

Tax office: www.sars.gov.za

Open a bank account: www.absa.co.za

Useful websites

Business guide: www.werksmans.co.za/sabusguide

Business news: www.cbn.co.za

The most widely read South African daily business newspaper: www.busrep.co.za

Tip

Why not take a look at South Africa's leading business, travel and tourism website at: www.mbendi.co.za

SPAIN

Spanish Embassy: www.spain.embassyhomepage.com

Chamber of Commerce: www.spanishchamber.co.uk/webenglish

Tax office: www.spainaccountants.com/tax.html

Where to go for advice on setting up a business:
www.idealspain.com/Pages/Information/business.htm

Open a bank account:
http://www.idealspain.com/Pages/finances/banks.asp

Useful websites

Business Spanish online: www.businessspanish.com

Guide to Spanish business letter writing:
www.englishspanishlink.com

A guide to Spanish business etiquette:
http://www.executiveplanet.com/business–etiquette/Spain.html

Tip

A great site for legal advice in Spain at:
www.spanish–town–guides.com/Legal_Advice_Spain.htm

SWEDEN

Swedish Embassy: www.swedish–embassy.org.uk

Chamber of Commerce: www.swedish–chamber.org.uk

Tax office:
http://www.skatteverket.se/ (in Swedish)
http://www.skatteverket.se/english/main/withhol.4.34a801ea1041d54f9e28000452.html

Where to go for advice on setting up a business:
www.sweden.se/templates/cs/BasicFactsheet____6755.aspx

Open a bank account:
www.sweden.se/templates/cs/Print_Article____5022.aspx

Useful websites

Reports on doing business in Sweden:
www.worldbiz.com/index.php/cPath/122

Sweden's business register:
www.scb.se/templates/Listning1____19852.asp

Free advice for foreign investors: www.isa.se

Tip

Here's a super list of Swedish business contacts: www.mkb.se/english/engsbc.htm

SWITZERLAND

Swiss Embassy: www.eda.admin.ch/london_emb/e/home.htm

Chamber of Commerce:
www.bscc.co.uk/DesktopDefault.aspx/tabid–1/294_read–2005

Tax office: www.estv.admin.ch/data/ist/e/vorzug.htm

Swiss Federal Tax Office:
http://www.efd.admin.ch/index.html?lang=en

Open a bank account: www.swiss–bank–accounts.com

Useful websites

Myths about Swiss bank accounts: www.swiss–bank–accounts.com/e/banking/7myths.html

FAQ's about swiss banking: www.swconsult.ch/chbanks/faq.htm

Living in Switzerland:
www.eda.admin.ch/london_emb/e/home/trach/resid.html

Tip

Discover the facts and the fictions behind a Swiss bank account at: www.howtoadvice.com/SwissBanks

THAILAND

Thai Embassy: thailand.embassyhomepage.com

British Chamber of Commerce: www.bccthai.com

Tax office: www.thaivisa.com/thailand_income_tax.0.html

Advice on setting up a business: www.thaivisa.com/314.0.html

Open a bank account: www.asiatradingonline.com/banks.htm

Useful websites

Banking advice:
www.bangkokbank.com/Bangkok+Bank/Personal+Banking/Foreign+Customers/Frequently+Asked+Questions.htm

Tip

An excellent website for corporate and legal advice at: www.businessmissionasia.com/corporateliaison.htm

TURKEY

Turkish Embassy: www.turkishembassy.org

Chamber of Commerce:
www.dalilusa.com/resource_center/turkish_chambers_commerce.asp

Information on Turkish tax liability:
www.expatfocus.com/expatriate–turkey–taxation

Open a bank account: www.turkishbanks.com/page/index.php

Useful websites

Advice on business etiquette:
www.executiveplanet.com/business–etiquette/Turkey.html

Turkish business directory:
www.turkish–media.com/en/tur_bus_dir.htm

Tip

It's not all work, work, work. Check out this excellent cultural site:
www.turkishconnection.com

UNITED ARAB EMIRATES

UAE Embassy: www.unitedarabemirates.embassyhomepage.com

Chamber of Commerce: www.adcci–uae.com

Tax office: www.dubai.usconsulate.gov/dubai/irs.html

Advice on setting up a business:
www.uaeinteract.com/business/settingup.asp

Open a bank account: www.icicibank.com/pfsuser/icicibank/ibank–nri/nrinewversion/uaehome.htm

Useful websites

Business directory: www.uaebusinessdirectory.com

Business guide: www.uae.org.ae/business/contents.htm

Tip

A great regional news source at: www.khaleejtimes.com/index00.asp

UNITED STATES OF AMERICA

US Embassy: www.usembassy.org.uk

Chamber of Commerce: www.uschamber.com

Tax office: www.treas.gov/offices/tax–policy

Advice on setting up a business: www.sba.gov

Open a bank account: www.usbank.com

Useful websites

Link to business centre: www.state.gov/business

Great link to US business news: www.newslink.org/biznews.html

Business statistics from the US census: www.census.gov/epcd/www/smallbus.html

American small business advisers www.score.org

Tip

An excellent site to guide you through the maze of rules and regulations involved in setting up a business in the USA at: www.business.gov

MORE RESOURCES

Books

Parfitt, J *Find Your Passion,* Lean Marketing Press

Parfitt, J and Tillyard, J *Grow Your Own Networks,* Lean Marketing Press

Parfitt, J *Career in Your Suitcase 3,* Lean Marketing Press

Griffiths, R and Kaday, C *Grow Your own Carrot,* Help Yourself

Head, S *How to Avoid a Near Life Experience,* HeadStart UK

Devalia, A *Get the Life you Love and Live it,* Nirvana Publishing

Burch, G *Go it Alone!,* Capstone Publishing Ltd

Southon, M, West, C *The Beermat Entrepreneur,* Prentice Hall

Kiyosaki, R *Rich Dad Poor Dad,* Imported Little, Brown USA titles

Sinetar, M *Do What You Love and the Money Follows,* Dell

Leboeuf, M *The Perfect Business,* Simon & Schuster

Darling, D *The Networking Survival Guide,* McGraw–Hill Higher Education

Risner, N *You Had Me At Hello,* Forest Oak Publications

Craven, R *Kick–Start Your Business,* Virgin Books

Kent, S *Odd Jobs,* Kogan Page

Crainer, S, Coomber, S and Dearlove, D *The Career Adventurer's Fieldbook,* Wiley

Kruempelmann, E *The Global Citizen,* Ten Speed Press

Gerber, M *The E–myth Revisted,* HarperCollins

Organisations	
Richard D Lewis	www.crossculture.com
Farnham Castle	www.farnhamcastle.com
Expatica	www.expatica.com
Websites	
Make the break	www.makethebreak.com
Get clients now	www.getclientsnow.com
Early to rise	www.earlytorise.com
Giveyourself a break	www.giveyourselfabreak.com
Jobsandmoms	www.jobsandmoms.com
Ezine help	
Just add Content	www.Justaddcontent.co.uk
Constant Contact	www.constantcontact.com
Aweber	www.aweber.com
Ezine queen	www.ezinequeen.com
Networks	
Ecademy	www.ecademy.com
TalentedWomen	www.talentedwomen.com
Linked In	www.linkedin.com

Printed in the United Kingdom
by Lightning Source UK Ltd.
112329UKS00001B/133-135

9 781905 43013